Praise for A Kosher Dating Odyssey

"The perfect mixture of self-deprecating humor and introspection."

—Hilary Daninhirsch, ForeWord Digital Reviews

"A humorous exploration of cross-faith dating, *A Kosher Dating Odyssey* is a strong pick for any humor, memoir or relationship collection."

—Midwest Book Review/Small Press Bookwatch

"Van Wallach's candid memoir, *A Kosher Dating Odyssey: One Former Texas Baptist's Quest for a Naughty and Nice Jewish Girl* is at once a sentimental education and a search for an intimate, fulfilling spirituality that will resonate with readers. His often amusing story is also uniquely American, shaped by the competing yet complementary forces of a multicultural journey from South Texas by way of France to the East Coast."

—Cora Monroe, Associate Professor of French, University of Puerto Rico at Mayagüez

"A big fat schmear of self-awareness on wry ... Wallach's 'date or die' persistence to find his b'shert deserves kudos. Between the Cuban yarmulkes, the Brazilian caiprinhas, and the West Village heartaches, this globe-trotting, found-again, smart but short Jew manages to put the 'sch' back into 'Men.'

"A rich book bigger than dating. A heart-felt search for roots, faith, soul and connection …

"Through an online Odyssean-style search to find his Jewish match, Wallach somehow manages to carve deep self-esteem out of multiple rejection. How refreshing! How revealing! But thank God he finally found her. Otherwise, he'd still be a menace online!!

"A heart-felt book that makes a gal reconsider her worst brush-off lines."

—Pamela Bloom, author of *Brazil Up Close* and *The Power of Compassion: Stories that Open the Heart, Heal the Soul and Change the World*

"As you might expect from a guy who has evolved from a Southern Baptist to a New England Jew, Van Wallach delivers a witty and unique tale of spiritual and romantic searching. But there's nothing more universal than love, and just about everyone will identify with his clever yarns spanning everything from the down-home to the erudite. With his ever-present and self-effacing sense of humor, Van 'looks for love in all the wrong places'—and some of the right ones."

—Stephen Hughes, Voice Artist and Writer

"In its own charming, awkward, and unwittingly honest way, *A Kosher Dating Odyssey* explores the complicated overlapping layers of finding Jewish identity, surviving decades of dating with an intact sense of humor, and whether the Internet helps or hurts our chances of finding true love on the flat screen. You would hardly think these topics would come together as seamlessly as they do. This is the brilliance of Van Wallach. Without adding even a sprinkle of gut-wrenching drama, overwrought navel-gazing or excessive self-pity—all of which would be perfectly justifiable—Wallach wins over the heart of his reader the same way he eventually gets the girl. By getting up to the plate over and over, and swinging the bat, figuring a home run is inevitable. You just can't help but root for the underdog, and secretly, see some part of yourself in every line."

—Monica Day, Founder, The Sensual Life; Host, "Essensuality: An Evening of Erotic Expression," and Creator, "The Essensual Experience: A Journey of Authentic Sensual Expression"

A Kosher Dating Odyssey

A Kosher Dating Odyssey:

One Former Texas Baptist's Quest for a Naughty & Nice Jewish Girl

Van Wallach

coffeetownpress
Seattle, WA

Published by Coffeetown Press
PO Box 70515
Seattle, WA 98127

For more information go to:
www.coffeetownpress.com
wallach.coffeetownpress.com

Cover design by Sabrina Sun

A Kosher Dating Odyssey: One Former Texas Baptist's Quest for a Naughty & Nice Jewish Girl

Portions of this book previously appeared in JDate's JMag, Blogcritics, Kesher Talk, Gringoes.com, The Princeton Alumni Weekly, The Daily Princetonian, and The Forward.

ISBN: 978-1-60381-132-3 (Trade Paper)
ISBN: 978-1-60381-133-0 (eBook)

Library of Congress Control Number: 2011944487
10 9 8 7 6 5 4 3 2 1
Printed in the United States of America

For my mother, Shirley Lissner Wallach, Shira bat Yared v'Chava, 1920-1984. May her memory be a blessing.

Contents

Chapter 1

Shards of Faith, Reassembled

I wear a *chai*—the Jewish letter symbolizing life—around my neck. I've studied Hebrew and Yiddish and have visited Israel. I subscribe to Jewish newspapers and have been told I look rabbinical; in fact, my great-great-grandfather, Heinrich (Chayim) Schwarz, was the first ordained rabbi in Texas.

Reading my religious résumé, you would never guess that I began my spiritual journey as a New Testament-reading, hell-fearing member of the First Baptist Church of Mission, Texas. How the heck, so to speak, did that happen? And how did I return to Judaism, which decades later led me to the whirling world of Jewish online dating?

The story started with my mother's German ancestors moving to the United States in 1854. The earliest direct ancestor to get the hell out of Europe was my great-great-grandfather Adolph Lissner, who landed in New York in time to serve in the Civil War. A death notice in the *New York Times* (January 21, 1914) says he was eighty-four years old and "one of the oldest Free Masons, being a member of the Emmanuel Lodge since 1855. Mr. Lissner served during the civil war with Troop E, Third Regiment, New York Cavalry." I found more in the New York municipal archives. He had died of pneumonia. He was the son of Samuel and Eva (Levine) Lissner. Following Jewish tradition, the names Samuel and Eva would surface in the generations flowing from Adolph. In fact, Adolph named his son, born in 1857, Samuel. The name carries over from generation to generation, *l'dor v'dor,* in Hebrew.

The Schwarz family—another band of plucky Prussians, as I like to call them—got its start in the U.S. in 1848, when Gabriel Schwarz moved to New York and then on to Charleston, S.C. Other family members followed, gravitating toward Texas. The book *Jewish Stars in Texas: Rabbis and Their Work* opens with a chapter on Rabbi Schwarz and his family and even features a photograph of the Rabbi Schwarz with his white beard and penetrating gaze on the cover.

My great-great-grandfather was the last Schwarz brother to pass over the Atlantic, leaving Posen, Germany and settling in Hempstead, Texas in 1873 with his wife Julia and five children, including fifteen-year-old Valeria. She would eventually marry Samuel Lissner. Their son, Jared, born in 1885, would be my grandfather. And Jared married Eva Michelson, daughter of German immigrants Lehman and Esther (Bath) Michelson. Their daughter Shirley Elizabeth, my mother, was born in Del Rio, Texas, on the banks of the Rio Grande, in 1920.

The Schwarzes and the Lissners typified the mid-nineteenth-century German Jewish wave of immigrants. They settled in small towns across Texas such as Hempstead, Marshall, Lockhart and especially Gonzales, where family members lived from the 1890s to the 1970s. Indeed, Gonzales had enough Jewish density to warrant two Jewish cemeteries. The one on Water Street contains the graves of the Michelsons, the Lissners, my mother, cousins and aunts and uncles. I try to visit Water Street whenever I'm in central Texas, along with Lockhart's Kreuz Market for messy, finger-licking good barbecue.

My mother's grave in Gonzales.

That's my mother's background. My father's family followed the arc of the next generation of immigrants. At the turn of the century they bolted out of Ukraine and other parts of Czar Nicholas II's creaky, Jew-hating empire, settling in St. Louis. My grandfather, blessed with the unpronounceable name of Isadore Sribnovolace (evidently Russian for "silverhair"), was born in 1899 in the shtetl of Vishnivitz. The last name was changed to Wallace when the family reached the United States. According to family lore, my grandfather tired of being beat up for having a Christian name, so he changed it to the more Jewish-sounding "Wallach" (fun fact: the original name of Maxim Litvinov, Joseph Stalin's foreign minister, was Meir Wallach).

The Germans and the Russians at my parents' wedding, 1955: McAllen. Left to right: Jared Lissner, Eva Lissner, Rhea Wallach, Edwin Wallach.

The derivation of the name, I've discovered, goes in several directions. In German, "Wallach" means gelding, which doesn't resonate with me. Wallachia is also a region in Romania. I fancy my roots go back to the vampires, but they don't. My favorite explanation comes from the Wallachs UNITE group on Facebook, where somebody wrote, perhaps after a few shots of Slivovitz kosher plum brandy:

> Yo wallachs a jewish name. Wallach. Its hebrew abreviation for Veyahavta Leraicha kamocha. id get out the whole hebrew letters but im 2 lazy. So anywayz, that means love ur neighbor like yourself. so yeah hebrew sounding person its hebrew lmao. heard that from my rabbi :D"

My mother met my father on a blind date in San Antonio in the mid 1950s. Both were Jewish, spoke English and had served in World War II. My father was on Okinawa, my mother was a Navy WAVE who served as a cryptographer in Washington, D.C., down the hall from Admiral William

Halsey. When President Roosevelt died in 1945, she supposedly had the duty of flashing the news to the Navy. So the story goes.

Other that these factual overlaps I can discern no psychic or social similarities between my parents—my mother, the plain-spoken daughter of small-town Texas, and my father, a big-city dreamer from St. Louis. They married in March of 1955 in Temple Emanuel in McAllen, Texas, the city east of Mission with an established Jewish population. They soon moved to France so my father could pursue a career in the auto industry while working on a U.S. Air Force base. Their union produced two sons.

As in other spheres of European life, the Russians and the Germans couldn't get along, so my mother returned to her hometown of Mission on the Mexican border—population 12,000 at the time, ninety percent Hispanic and founded in 1908. A hot, flat, primarily agricultural town. I have no memories of us together as a family, just a flashback to a car ride before Dad left. They had split up when she moved to Mission. My father remarried and moved to Michigan and then New York. My brother and I saw him one weekend in ten years, between 1962 and 1972. It was September 1970, when I should have been having the bar mitzvah I never had. He was forty-five—nine years younger than I am now.

While my father's family, which I would not get to know until I was an adult, stayed Jewish, my mother's family intermarried with Christians and converted over the generations. Her sister Charlotte married a Baptist man in the late 1930s, and she became a devout member of the Green Acres Baptist Church of Tyler, Texas, east of Dallas. Intermarriage made practical sense for Jewish families isolated in small communities and surrounded by evangelica[l] Christians, who enjoyed nothing so much as sharing the[ir] hellfire-and-damnation vision with members of the Tribe of Abraham. Why, they got heavenly brownie points for converting us! I imagine it took a sturdy, ornery devotion to Judaism to withstand the social pressure to fit in.

My mother, Shirley, had a sturdy and ornery side. Shards of her Jewishness are lodged in my earliest memories. While my mother had no outward interest in any faith, she had bucked the family trend toward intermarriage and then provided, for reasons I cannot fathom, some aspects of a Jewish home after my parents split up. I had not even turned three. I like to think that a spark of the *neshama* (the Hebrew word for "soul"), of Rabbi Schwarz of Hempstead remained in her, which she unconsciously passed along. Once we went to Temple Emanuel in McAllen, although my brother Cooper and I didn't like it. Mom taught us the essential Jewish prayer, the *Sh'ma*. We had a menorah in the house and two books: the *Union Prayer Book* and *The Wit and Wisdom of the Talmud*, printed in the 1920s. Mom kept a bottle of Manischewitz concord grape wine in the refrigerator, forever skewing my taste toward nauseatingly sweet kosher wines. I remember Mom sobbing when she watched *Judgment at Nuremberg* on TV. She saved her *ketubah,* or Jewish wedding contract. But we never had a Shabbat dinner, a *seder* (festive meal at home for the observance of Passover), or Hanukkah celebrations. An unexplained rift with the Jewish community in McAllen cut off almost all contact with other Jews in the area. A Jewish man owned Joe's Army Store across the railroad tracks on South Conway Avenue, but Mom refused to speak to him, perhaps because of disagreements over how she should be raising us. Two sisters who lived in McAllen—Fanny and Lena—always gave us gingerbread cookies for Hanukkah. That's the extent of my memories of the Jewish community. Rather than a faith, Judaism and the Jewish community evolved into a vague, ominous presence identified with my father and murky forces that made Mom unhappy.

The First Baptist Church of Mission in 2011, looking much as it did in the early 1960s.

Isolated and indifferent to Jewish practice, my mother left religious instruction to our Southern Baptist neighbor, Mrs. D. Her unwavering faith reflected the Baptists' enthusiastic love of and exasperated impatience with "the Jewish people" to make our family a natural target for intensive spiritual cultivation. Every Sunday, Cooper and I were delivered to the First Baptist for Sunday School, and in the summer we attended Vacation Bible School. My favorite VBS memory: making a shoeshine box with wood that I lovingly sanded and varnished. At Sunday School in the fall and winter, my class devoted as much time to scoping the day's Dallas Cowboys game as to the teachings of the Good Book. Coach Tom Landry, after all, was a Mission native, and his father Ray had been the fire chief and still operated Landry's Garage. Still, enough of the Gospel message seeped into my open mind to have an impact. No Jewish influence existed to provide an alternative viewpoint or to buck up any contrary awareness. My father never visited, and his parents—retired since the late 1940s to Coral Gables and Miami Beach—ignored us.

For male role models, I had the pastors of the First Baptist. I remember them as decent, caring, even learned men who went easier on the hellfire than the traveling evangelists who held spirit-flaying crusades in the Rio Grande Valley. Brother Dugger, Brother Glenn and Brother Buddy—good guys all of them, visiting the sick and listening to the troubled. I especially like to remember Brother Glenn McCollum, father of an elementary school classmate and an avid collector of barbed wire. I guess that's a Texas thing. Their offices at the FBC, bookshelves loaded with Greek and Hebrew texts, fascinated me. I wonder what might have happened had I had followed up on my lingering glances at those language texts and asked to learn some Hebrew. As a bona fide member of the Chosen People, I had the right to know—and it would serve a practical purpose, strengthening my ability to discuss the irrefutable proofs of Christianity with Jewish relatives. As it was, the only Hebrew I knew came from reading a Harry Kemelman mystery novel, which featured a character named Rabbi David Small. The book said that the Hebrew letters for "kosher" looked a little like "7WD" in English, so I could always identify that word.

My search for identity in an overwhelming non-Jewish world flowed toward Christian belief. I struggled under a triple sense of isolation: I was Jewish, a gringo and the offspring of divorced parents. I would grasp at anything that offered a mainstream identity. Looking back, I can see how I craved group membership, something beyond the negatives I associated with my childhood reality. Christianity offered a way out of the gnawing aloneness, even as it caused its own anxieties. From a young age, the hellfire messages of Baptist preachers terrified me into unease, guilt and finally acquiescence. To relieve the gnawing fear of damnation, I accepted Jesus and was duly baptized on Super Bowl Sunday, 1972. That's also the day the beloved Dallas Cowboys—coached by Mission's own hometown Christian gentleman, Tom Landry—beat the Miami Dolphins 24-3. Thank you, Lord! I became annoyingly devout, desperate for direction and acceptance in life.

And yet ... we remained the town Jews. My mother's family moved from Del Rio to Mission in 1925, only seventeen years after the town was founded; everybody knew who and what we were. Mrs. D called Cooper and me her "Jew-els." When golf-obsessed Cooper wanted to join the Fellowship of Christian Athletes in high school, the adult sponsor exclaimed, "Why, Cooper, you can't join the FCA. You're a Jew!" In one surreal episode, my high school class trouped to a movie theater on the south side of town for a free showing of *Fiddler on the Roof.* Finally, a sense of connection! My mother donated to Israel relief efforts after the 1973 Yom Kippur War.

Meanwhile, a kernel of curiosity about our heritage sprouted in me. I listened to a San Antonio radio show, "The Christian-Jew Hour," that crackled 250 miles over the AM airwaves to reach Mission. I read literature from the so-called "Messianic Jews" to try to square the circle of irreconcilable belief systems. A Texas evangelist and Jewish convert, Irwin "Rocky" Freeman, held a crusade at the First Baptist and made a point of visiting our home. In retrospect, I can see I wanted to have my kugel and eat it, too.

The circle would be broken when Cooper and I finally visited our long-absent father in Manhattan for a week in 1972. A self-employed engineer and inventor, he attacked my religious beliefs and most aspects of our small-town Texas upbringing, which he loathed. The revulsion for all things Texas was part of his strong negative feelings toward our mother, which, of course, pushed us away from him every time he opened his mouth. What teenager wants to hear a stranger attack the mother he loves? As a strategy for rebuilding any kind of father-son relationship, it completely failed. Still, in his ham-handed way, Dad showed me I didn't *have* to be a Baptist. He pried a few fingers from my death grip on the King James Bible. Doubts like weeds cracked the concrete of my faith as adolescence caused its own changes and doubts in life, as I became a mesquite-country version of Alexander Portnoy, with my own complaints. Bit by bit, I became disenchanted with the Christianity imposed on me. I slowly began to wonder about my Jewish heritage, how I could acknowledge it within rigid Baptist beliefs. I wrote a poem called "Jew-Boy" about my dilemma:

It's so hard to know why I am
So sad to be what I am
Strange for you to see who I am

I found myself on a swaying spiritual tightrope. I was creeping away from Christianity and the First Baptist but couldn't see how to move closer to Judaism. I had no Jewish friends and no Jewishly involved relatives nearby. I did get packages of articles and brochures on Judaism from my eccentric Aunt Pearl in Los Angeles, an opera-loving health food fanatic and sister of my grandfather in Miami Beach. My journal from the era records the defining moments on the tightrope, as I worked up the chutzpah required for a sixteen-year-old to go talk to a rabbi alone. On September 7, 1974—shortly after Cooper and I spent several weeks with our father in New York and also in Miami Beach, where we met our grandparents Edwin and Rhea for the first and only time since we were infants—I wrote:

> I have temporarily concluded that to be a Jew, one must *be* a Jew. It's not a Jew-when-it-suits-me proposition. It's neither sinful nor wrong to accept my heritage; indeed, it might be my destiny to accept it. Perhaps it is the end of a journey. I am out of place at the FBC of Mission. Something doesn't fit. I have forced myself to face the facts. Like Dad said, I can't run away from what I am.

Soon, I tested my emerging identity on a high school classmate, the late Lena Guerrero, who as an adult become a rising star in national politics and the Texas Railroad Commissioner, until her misstatements about her college transcript wrecked her public-sector career in 1992. Anytime we interacted was a big deal for me, and I recorded this conversation with Lena:

> "I still have to call the rabbi when I get home," I said.
>
> "Wooow!" replied Lena.
>
> "I've been thinking about stuff like that recently. I guess I'd better. I just want to talk with him. I'm pretty confused."
>
> "You're a Baptist, aren't you?" she asked.
>
> "Yes, but I've been feeling strange there. Seems like all I do is keep a chair warm on Sunday mornings. I'm a little fed up with the FBC. I don't know why."

On September 14, 1974, my mother drove me to McAllen's Temple Emanuel, where I met Rabbi Maynard. I spoke generally about my background, my late grandparents who had lived in Mission for over thirty years, but I could never admit that I had accepted Christianity. Raw, scabrous guilt over colliding faiths silenced me. I felt like a fraud among the Jews and a backslider among the Baptists, with nobody to consult about my doubts. Instead, I bore a self-applied mark of Cain. I swallowed my emotions and presented a wildly distorted history. I wrote:

> He showed me around the temple after giving me a yarmulke, which I kept. He showed me the Torah scrolls and the *Ner Tamid* [the "eternal lamp" that hangs above the scrolls]. After a tour, he asked me if I had any more questions, if he could be of any more help. I should have told him I had attended church for ten years, instead of telling him that I never got around to coming to the synagogue.

But the drive toward a new path propelled me onward. On September 17, I wrote,

> Monday marked another of the icebergs of existence, almost a multi-first. I WENT TO NOT ONLY MY FIRST SYNAGOGUE SERVICE BUT MY FIRST ROSH HASHANAH SERVICE. How's that for a dramatic announcement?
>
> I pumped up my courage and walked to the entrance. The door was held open—a good sign. I walked in. Unsure of the next step, I read the memorial plaques until an elderly woman came by. She asked me if I was waiting for anybody.
>
> "No, I'm, ah, visiting. Could you show the seating arrangement?" We entered the fellowship hall, as the good Baptists would say. I firmly—PROUDLY—put on the yarmulke. It felt quite natural, although as foreign to me in practice as wearing nylons.

Back home, my mother asked why I had been so secretive about going to the temple.

"I didn't think you cared," I told her.

"Don't say that, Van. You know I'm interested in everything you do. Can't you even talk to your own mother? Don't you trust me?"

I had no reply for her. A week later I attended Yom Kippur services.

I was much more relaxed this time. I even struck up a conversation with a woman who was a convert from Catholicism. She seemed to understand my circumstances. She even said, "You must be lonely."

"You're so right, lady, so right," I wrote in my journal.

Temple Emanuel in McAllen, since relocated to a new building.

I stopped going to church but lacked the strength to start going to temple, although the leader of the youth group called me once, a thoughtful gesture. By 1975 my identity and belief as a Southern Baptist vanished. The Baptist faith simply didn't work for me, and I was no longer going to pretend it did. Lacking any support or guidance, I started down a wandering path of personal reinvention. My Jewish self-education started as I read books like *This is My God* by Herman Wouk, *Exodus* by Leon Uris and *Basic Judaism* by Milton Steinberg. I liked what I read about Judaism—the faith's simplicity and self-acceptance versus the devouring anxiety I felt as a Christian, where I always wondered if I measured up to perfection, whether I *truly* believed.

Trust me on this: Jewish guilt is nothing compared to the fears of a doubting evangelical. The last time I ever attended the First Baptist was as a high school senior in 1976—to get a graduation Bible. They wanted to give me one, and simple civility led me to accept it.

I didn't realize then that friends also had questions and crises of faith over the decades. They made profound changes that broke from family traditions: Catholic to Mormon, Christian Scientist to Catholic, Catholic to Unitarian .... Even the Protestants—Baptists and Methodists—switched around to find their right church homes. As far as I know, I was the only one jotting notes on the journey.

I made other life-changing decisions at the same time. I worked as a paid reporter for Mission's weekly newspaper, the *Upper Valley Progress*, bumbled through dating disasters with love interest Venus (discussed in the chapter "Baptist Chick in a Halter Top") and applied for colleges. College searches in the 1970s were more haphazard than today. I had always assumed I would attend the University of Texas at Austin, where everybody in my family went. Visions of writing for the *Daily Texan* danced in my head. So I applied there. On a whim I applied for a full scholarship from the University of Dallas, a Catholic school where I fancied majoring in classics, going so far as to teach myself the ancient Greek alphabet. I won one of the scholarships without even visiting the campus. Based on campus visits from the fateful summer of 1975 spent in New York with my father and his wife, I applied and won admission to Princeton and Columbia Universities. My twelve-page Princeton application essay had this gem of teenage ennui: "My little town, as Simon and Garfunkel dub it, of north side, railroad tracks, south side barrio, Anglo Protestants, Chicano Catholics, limited dating opportunities and bland educational facilities denoted a self-contained environment that bored me." Limited dating opportunities? They must have chuckled over that at the Admissions Office. But the essay helped get me in. I still remember when Mom brought the thick congratulatory envelope home from her office at Conway, Dooley & Martin Insurance Agency, where she was a secretary.

The Bicentennial summer of 1976 graced me with bittersweet memories of the twilight of my life in the Rio Grande Valley. My reporter gig with the *Progress* occupied me with writing and photography. I was dating another new graduate, a girl from McAllen High School (AKA McHi) whom I had met when in literary competitions. We enjoyed and suffered through a summer of the pure, nervous thrill of first-love explorations. That included listening to jazz albums (for teen intellectuals, a sure symptom of existentialist torment), hanging out at a festival in McAllen's Archer Park on the Fourth of July 1976, and watching the Summer Olympics, dominated by Sugar Ray Leonard and the invincible U.S. boxing team. As the summer spun on, the relationship faltered; I was heading east and she was staying in Texas for college. Plus, we both felt the religious gap between us, for I was upfront about my Judaism and she was a Methodist.

"Would you ever marry someone who wasn't Jewish?" she asked.

"No," I said.

In August I cut off my summer beard, grabbed a manual typewriter, donned my best leisure suit and shipped out to the mystery of college in the East. Princeton University was the first place I met Jews outside my family. I checked out Hillel activities during Freshman Week and signed up for Hillel classes. But while I had left the Baptists, they hadn't left me. My heritage dogged me, along with my utter lack of familiarity with Jewish practice and culture (watching *Annie Hall* and understanding the jokes doesn't count). I had never attended Hebrew school, never lit Hanukkah candles, never had a Shabbat dinner, never attended a Passover seder, never swung a Purim *grogger* (noisemaker). The Jews at Princeton seemed so East Coast smart and at ease, even jaded, in their faith. I felt shame at my ignorance. Book learning could not replace the experiential void. I yearned to know and be accepted, but I had no way of doing that. Like the simple son at the Passover seder, I did not know to ask. I thought about unburdening myself to the Hillel rabbi but he intimidated me. In fact, I saw all Jewish authority figures as echoes of my father, who would mock rather than understand me. Christianity remained my cross to bear. While my former beliefs held no appeal, I could not find a niche in Princeton's Jewish life. The few times I tried to attend services I felt completely befuddled and was sure I was the only one lacking total fluency with the prayers and Hebrew language.

My work as a reporter on *The Daily Princetonian* did bring me into contact with Jewish themes. My very first lead story as a freshman, from 1977, covered a speech by Nazi-hunter Simon Wiesenthal.

There had been one major shift in my orientation: from the moment I reached campus I irresistibly gravitated toward Jewish women. Even before classes started, I had a schoolboy crush on one I met on my Outdoor Action camping trip. Meeting Jewish women for the first time ever, I totally wanted to know them. However, in those early days of co-education at Princeton, the male-female ratio tilted horrendously four to one, so the odds were against my success with the opposite sex. My dismal relationship outlook was compounded by my social awkwardness and grievous sense of inadequacy. I still recall my very first class, Spanish 101 at 185 Nassau Street. The class composition: fifteen men and one (Jewish) woman.

Mom and me as I was leaving for Princeton in 1976, looking every inch the mid-70s fashion disaster.

I remember other classes, such as a Russian literature precept, for the learning experience and my hormonal attraction to the sultry Semitic instructors. I pined for one busty fellow student in particular. I finally got up the courage to tell her, as we walked through the vast lobby of Firestone Library, "I really like you."

"Oh, I like you too, Van, as a friend," she replied as I crumbled like stale matzoh into the polished floors of knowledge. (There is, I'm pleased to report, some justice in the world. This woman and I dated a bit after we graduated, and we still meet for lunch every couple of years.)

I was already writing about my dismal social life. From an early age, any adventure or mishap became fodder for a literary effort. In the summer of 1979 I was an intern feature writer for *Newsday,* the major Long Island newspaper. I longed for social connection that I lacked at Princeton during that summer of long lines at gas stations. My hapless search was detailed in the essay, "Fear and Loathing on the Long Island Singles Scene," in the September 12, 1979 issue of *The Daily Princetonian,* included as chapter 2.

Back on campus, Jewish holidays passed in silence. Nobody invited me home for seders. Had I been more involved in Hillel, willing to say those three hard little words —"I need help"—then maybe I would have been welcome somewhere. I never asked, and nobody bothered to read my mind. That changed in my senior year when classmates Marc and Steve invited me to join their families in Brooklyn and the Bronx for Passover. These friends helped me take my first steps into Jewish life. Marc and Steve both did great *mitzvahs* (worthy deeds) and I will always be grateful to them and their parents for welcoming a stranger into their midst.

The pace of Jewish exploration quickened when I moved to Brooklyn a week after graduating from Princeton. I had parlayed extensive but lightweight journalism experience and my economics degree into a job as a reporter-researcher at *Forbes* magazine. On the social-Judaic front, I was astounded by New York's density of Jewish institutions and Jewish women. While other college graduates hit the bars and discos, synagogue-hopping became my weekend obsession, as I sought to expand my Jewish experiences. I sampled everything from Reform temples to the Flatbush Minyan and for a while I attended the beginners' services at the orthodox Lincoln Square Synagogue. Rabbi Ephraim Buchwald, who led the services, was so impressive that I continue to follow his work at the National Jewish Outreach Program. At the Society for the Advancement of Judaism, part of the Reconstructionist movement, I wore a *tallis,* or prayer shawl, for the first time.

On the cultural side, I attended a presentation at New York University by Yiddish writer and Nobel Prize winner Isaac Bashevis Singer, who graciously autographed my copy of his book *The Family Moskat.* Expressing my strong desire for group identity, I attended rallies in New York and Washington to support the cause of Soviet Jewry and I still have a massive dry-mounted poster from a 1983 rally. On a hot August Sunday, I joined a Jewish singles group's outing to the Brighton Beach section of Brooklyn, where we saw that hilarious new movie, *Airplane.* Years later, a woman from the trip would identify me at a synagogue based on my Texas background and unusual name—those details did make me stand out.

My explorations were not aimless; I had chosen my path and never doubted my direction for a minute. The future wasn't the problem, rather, the unresolved past was gnawing at me. I could never talk about that past. I arrived at services eager and anxious, and seemingly from nowhere.

Only one negative bump occurred on my path to Jewish awareness. In the summer of 1981, while between jobs, I spent a weekend in Connecticut with an Orthodox group called Ohr Somayach. I had read its literature when representatives visited Princeton and I liked the idea of study and Hebrew learning. I fit the profile of people the group wished to target: college aged, interested in Judaism but lacking knowledge. That was me, and I must have looked like a big, juicy candidate for *baal teshuva* (returnee to Judaism) status. One of them tracked me down after I graduated and invited me to a weekend retreat. I agreed and traveled up by train. By that time I already identified with Conservative Judaism, in theory if not practice. The rabbi leading the weekend challenged my beliefs, which I couldn't really defend. As the weekend progressed, I felt more pressured to stay longer, although I had to return to New York and get ready for my new job.

Ohr Somayach couldn't have known, but the way it approached me was catastrophically wrong. I knew all about pressure to conform in a religious setting, and I resented anything resembling aggressive, in-your-face questioning of my evolving beliefs (I remember being badgered on the streets of New York by members of the Unification Church in the 1970s). A softer, more reasonable touch to engage me over the long term would have worked much better. But that's not the way it went down. I looked like a nail, so the rabbi reached for his hammer. He kept hassling me, and I kept digging my heels in just as I did years earlier when my father slammed my Christian beliefs. After a final one-on-one appeal with a "father-son" theme, the rabbi finally relented and I eagerly boarded the train back to New York. The episode disgusted me so much that when I got back to my apartment I cut off my beard to avoid looking anything like an Ohr Somayach type.

In 1982 I grew back my beard and visited Israel. Now, having studied Hebrew on and off for years, I belong to a Modern Orthodox shul. You could call me a do-it-yourself *baal teshuva*, or returnee to Judaism. Fortunately, my weekend with Ohr Somayach had only alienated me from Ohr Somayach, not from Judaism.

My Judaism and my Texas roots sometimes intersected. I began dating a prototypical "older woman" I met at Congregation Emunath Israel on West 23rd Street in 1981. I can still remember the event—a discussion by The Generation After, a group of children and descendants of

Holocaust survivors. In a big romantic gesture for this woman, I placed a small ad in the *Jewish World* newspaper, where I was freelancing, in April 1981 (SA refers to San Antonio, where she had lived once):

> Joanne: Kosher armadillos and barbequed lox—no place else but Brooklyn (and SA). Happy Pesach, Van.

I reflected on the changes in my life in my journal in this passage from June 7, 1981:

> I was up until 3 a.m. looking at vols. 2 and 3, digging into the Jewish passages. While they don't shed much light on my religious thinking per se (other passages more than express my Christian fervor of that long-ago age) they tell me, and you, that the Jewish spirit always burned close to the surface and forced me to acknowledge the anti-Jewishness of my surroundings ... I mean, I wrote about somebody saying, "We shoot Jews here" and left it without commentary. How did I feel about these events?

I always had a sense of history. The next day I noted,

> Something important happened today. Israel bombed an Iraqi H-Bomb (so they allege) plant and is now reaping the expected whirlwind of world condemnation. On one hand it's a brave, daring, to-hell-with-world-opinion move that flies in the face of old Jewish behavior. Of that I'm proud—it's the kind of preventive action America must shy away from. Yet, doubts remain. Would the Iraqis have

> really used H-bombs on Israel? Not hardly ... a tip of the beanie to you, Menachem. Let's just hope the world leaves you a place to hang it.

I started connecting with Jewish women. After a conversation at the Village Temple, I realized my circumstances had changed. I spoke with a woman after services, told her I was a new Princeton graduate, and she exclaimed, "You seem so together!"

Me? I thought, the guy who couldn't even get a date at Princeton?

Even as I started to assess the possibilities of a real social and religious life in New York, the Baptist past haunted me. How deeply that past remained embedded in me soon became obvious. The culture clash hit me hard when early-'80s love interest Calypso (discussed in a later chapter) and I saw Robert Duvall's movie *Tender Mercies.* In it, Duvall's character, a dissolute country-western singer, turns his life around through Christianity and the love of a good woman and is baptized. With my background, I found the scene moving—but the New York audience laughed. Look at the yokels!

Another time, I met a woman, Beth, who was Jewish, jolly, secular and from Long Island. She invited me to join carolers bringing holiday cheer to Brooklyn. I reluctantly agreed and we gathered one Saturday. Was the first song "Jingle Bells"? I don't remember. What I do recall is a sudden choking feeling. A wave of anxiety washed over me as I realized, *I can't do this.* The songs all had personal significance and childhood associations far beyond secular celebration.

"I'm sorry, I have to leave," I told Beth as I hurried away.

I called her later to explain. Beth had no personal connection to the songs, but for me they reflected a faith I had been raised in and rejected, one that affirmed the birth of the Savior. To this day I do not sing or listen to holiday music—whether the topic is Jesus, a white Christmas or Rudolph the Red-Nosed Reindeer.

I finally settled on the conservative Kane Street Synagogue in Brooklyn as my spiritual home. I still recall my first Saturday morning service. I knew so little about Jewish customs that I recoiled and shook my head when a man offered me the honor of an *aliyah* during the Torah reading. During an *aliyah*, you read prayers in Hebrew before and after parts of the weekly recitation from the Jewish Bible. I had no idea what to do, so I declined. Who was I to deserve this? What if I screwed up?

I had reached an impasse. Spiritually, I was at ease in Jewish beliefs and had no desire to go backward, but I saw no way forward without 'fessing up to my ignorance and what I viewed as my twisted background. I finally decided to speak with Kane Street's rabbi, a man I liked immensely. In this Jewish version of a confessional, I came clean—about my parents, the Baptist beliefs, the unguided drift from Christianity to Judaism, my sense of shame at what I had been.

To my surprise and delight, the rabbi expressed not the least bit of shock. He didn't chuck me out of his office. It turns out that I'm not the first Jew to lack a bar mitzvah or an enriching Jewish upbringing. Imagine that. Our conversation marked my fresh start as a Jew. As the Baptists would say, I got right with God. I was relieved to have faced the facts of the past without being laughed at.

Over the last thirty years, I have built my version of a Jewish life. I have studied Hebrew and have become, if not fluent, then more aware of what's happening during services. I studied Yiddish at the Workmen's Circle; I cemented my commitment to the class by walking over the Brooklyn Bridge on the Fourth of July, 1982, to buy the classic textbook, *College Yiddish,* by Uriel Weinreich (being who I am, I wrote the date inside the book). In 1982 I also visited Israel for the first and, so far, only time, writing an essay about my experiences in what was then the *Jewish Daily Forward* newspaper, when it published an English-language weekend section:

> [Our group arrived at the Wall Friday afternoon, the beginning of Shabbat. We noticed a swirl of activity.] It was a phalanx of young men, clad in white shirts, coming to welcome the Sabbath. While I did not have the foggiest idea of the literal meaning of their song, its emotion was evident. The solidarity and presence of the group deeply moved me. In that twilight Jerusalem moment, I grasped an essential element of Jewishness in Israel. There was a sense of communal holiness among people bound together in their own land, freed from interpreting their lives in relation to a dominant, assimilating culture.

Our guide's live-and-let-live attitude impressed me. Speaking about the Israelis' relaxed approach to religious practice, Benny pointed at the Wall and declared, "*This* is our spirituality."

After years of dating around, I met a woman I deeply cared for and connected with, as two creative outsiders in the city. We were married under the *chuppah*, or wedding canopy, at the Kane Street Synagogue in 1989 by a new rabbi, a woman I like to call "Rebbe Debbie." In another cultural mash-up, the klezmer band hired for the wedding played Ernest Tubb's "Waltz Across Texas" as the first dance. Has a klezmer band ever attempted a Texas honky-tonk classic so gamely? I doubt it. Let's call the performance a noble experiment and leave it at that.

My wife and I took *ulpan*, or intensive Hebrew, when we considered moving to Israel, a plan cut short by the start of Gulf War I. (Playing our relocation slightly safer, we moved to Connecticut.) Since my divorce in 2003, I have dated Jewish women almost exclusively, finding them intelligent, passionate and adorable. The rhythms of Judaism seeped into me, so that I transferred the emotional response I had to Christian prayers and music to Jewish liturgy that I have heard hundreds of times—*Aleiynu, Adon Olam, Yedid Nefesh, Ain Keloheynu, Kaddish* and Israel's national anthem, *Hatikva*. The writings of Rabbi Abraham Twerski, who is also a psychiatrist, gave me comfort during years of stress, as did the book *Jewish Meditation* by the late Rabbi Arye Kaplan. I still turn to both of them for guidance. My adult experiences are catching up to the intellectual leap I made as a teenager.

I gave myself the Hebrew name *Ze'ev* (wolf) to use in synagogue events and language classes. In 2010 I joined Beit Chaverim (House of Friends), a Modern Orthodox synagogue in Connecticut. At the age of fifty-three, I finally figured out how to put on *tefillin*, the leather straps for your arm and head. The straps hold boxes with biblical verses and are worn during morning prayers. I'm now trying to lead a less digitally driven life on *Shabbat*, primarily by not signing in to email or Facebook. It gets easier, although I sometimes give in to the Devil and backslide into old habits. Oops, there I go again with the Baptist terminology.

While I've made peace with my past and current beliefs, I am still aware of the split in my life. My Jewish friends remember childhood seders; I remember Easter egg hunts. They played with *dreydls* (the spinning tops used for gambling for chocolate coins at Hanukkah), I decorated Christmas trees. They hated Hebrew school, I liked Vacation

Bible School. My childhood and adult sides are mostly separate. These worlds collide on Facebook, where secular Jewish friends from Princeton and Israel encounter my evangelical friends from Texas and their straight-talking professions of belief. Their views on faith differ sharply. My attitude? You're all big boys and girls; you can sort out your differences. But I am tickled to be in the middle, seeing people from the opposite poles of my life interacting.

The chasm yawned widest whenever I returned to Mission in the 1980s and visited with Mrs. D. My change saddened her. "Could you ever believe the way you used to?" she once asked.

"No," I said. "I'm happy with who I am now."

To this day, my evangelical friends and relatives will try to win me back over to the Christian team. One cousin wrote, "I'd be curious to know your thoughts on the Old Testament prophecies of the Messiah to come. I believe Jesus is the fulfillment of those prophecies."

I responded, "As far as the Old Testament prophecies, I used to think the way you do, but I gradually changed my mind and think of them on their own, with Jewish meanings that differ from the Christian interpretation." I then directed her to the group Jews for Judaism, which counteracts missionary efforts aimed at Jews.

Christian pitches never work now because I am at peace with my Jewish beliefs and don't care to engage in fierce theological disputes based on their interpretation of the so-called Old Testament. They can call up every possible "proof text" of fulfilled prophecies and logic arguments pointing to Christianity, and I politely demur. However, I'm never insulted or even bothered by their efforts, because I understand that they are motivated by faith. Each one is a dedicated salesperson, driven to make a pitch and ask for the sale.

Some shards of faith, old and new, bridge the distance of

decades. As a mirror of my personality, the transition from conservative Christianity to conservative Judaism makes perfect sense; new-fangled forms of spiritual expression never worked for me. Indeed, I joke that if I were a Catholic, I'd learn Latin and grumble in favor of the Tridentine Mass.

Like a good Baptist, I watch my language. You'll rarely hear what we quaintly called "cuss" words pass my lips. The importance of Bible reading remains in me, so I try to keep up with the *perek yomi* (Torah chapter of the day) program published by the Orthodox Union, although now I limit my scriptural readings to the, ahem, Old Testament. I have faith in faith and don't spend much time in agonized arguments with God about His existence, mercy or common sense. He is what He is. Community engagement matters, so I attend synagogue when I can, bringing my post-bar mitzvah son along so he can round out the ten-man *minyan,* that is, the group of men required to say certain prayers at Orthodox services. I truly feel as if we're contributing. Through Facebook, I've connected with Jewish relatives in Texas, other members of the far-scattered Schwarz clan.

Politically, I lack the intense anger many of my Northeastern and/or liberal friends feel toward evangelicals; I may disagree with the Christians' views, but I understand where they're coming from and I keep the differences on the political level. I know enough to subdue my maverick political and economic views around certain liberal friends, lest their eyes bug out in disbelief and they dump bowls of boiling matzoh ball soup on me.

On the Jewish front, I have the family menorah and the Union Prayer Book from Mission, and historical books on Texas Jews mentioning that hardy Prussian on the prairie, Rabbi Schwarz. Mrs. D gave me her wonderful antique edition of *The Works of Flavius Josephus,* inscribed with the date, December 30, 1916. Ornate formal photographs from the 1890s of my great-grandparents, Esther and Lehman Michelson, have pride of place in my apartment. The *chai* worn around my neck? Mom gave it to me for Hanukkah, 1979, four years before she died of cancer. While a Baptist preacher presided over my mother's funeral and she was cremated, her older sister Charlotte, a fervent Baptist, placed her tombstone in the Jewish cemetery in Gonzales, Texas, next to their parents' graves. My son had the bar mitzvah I never had, and my brother and his son Tyler were among the honored guests. Whenever I'm in McAllen, I attend services at Temple Emanuel—where I feel most welcome. And I still say the *Sh'ma* every night, the way my mother taught me.

With my brother Cooper at my son's bar mitzvah.

Chapter 2

Fear and Loathing on the Long Island Singles Scene

[In the summer of 1979, between my junior and senior years at Princeton University, I had a plum job as an intern feature writer for *Newsday*, a major daily based in Garden City, New York. After the summer I wrote this piece for the September 12, 1979 issue of *The Daily Princetonian*, for incoming freshmen. The anxiety in the piece about driving and gasoline reflected the gas crisis of that summer, which led to long lines at gas stations. My harebrained efforts to conserve gas and limit driving in my 1971 AMC Hornet put me into ridiculous situations. I've added bracketed explanatory notes to flesh out the last thirty-three years of life experience. Looking back, I'm surprised that I didn't put any effort into Jewish dating events—but I did attend one at a church.]

Once school had ended last spring, but before my summer as a reporter on Long Island began, I immediately immersed myself in the cathode hot tub of American culture. On any evening in early June I hunkered down in front of Colonial Club's TV, deliciously slack-jawed while advertisements played the summer hard sell, showering this winter shut-in with scenes of beach frolic, the open road and heavy, heavy socializing.

The message fit nicely with the brochures sent to the

Newsday interns. TV said *what* to do, while the booklets and maps told me *where* to do it. (With *whom* was the problem.) Equipped with my first car, the Newsday social calendar and, of course, lots of gasoline, I was bound and determined to enjoy myself, even if I nearly killed myself in the process.

My main outlet for this urge was the Long Island singles scene. Various groups ran notices in *Newsday*, and, as a total stranger to such activities, I decided to investigate some of them. Beneath my thoughts then was an image of the mythical summer romance, a way of celebrating and sharing the first season of being truly independent.

As things transpired, Murphy's Law—if something can go wrong, it will—became the organizing principle of my adventures, as the bubble of expectations shrank rapidly after continual prickings. Like a surfer who paddles farther and farther out to sea in search of the perfect wave, I wasted a lot of time looking for something that wasn't there, while missing the lesser but more accessible possibilities for diversion. Once I shed the Mr. Goodbar mentality, things improved. There's nothing wrong with watching the Yankees with neighbors.

So there were lessons to be learned, or relearned in some cases, over the summer. Mainly, I realized that in life, unlike sports, you don't have to score to win. To make a deliberate search for the love of your life—whether at singles' bars or their collegiate equivalent, club parties—is an exercise in futility. Friends are made, not captured.

Freshmen should keep that in mind as they pass through the swirl of introductions and forgotten names this week. More than high grades or a superficial social visibility, the friends you make and the experiences you share will give Princeton a meaning and fullness that will remain with you long after academic matters have slipped into the past. [Incredibly enough, this pathetic attempt to rationalize socio-sexual failure turned out to be true.]

Different adventures yielded different lessons. For freshmen and others who prefer to experience such things vicariously, the following vignettes should suffice.

You're your own best transportation. You invite disaster when you must rely upon the good will of other people to meet your transportation needs. Nobody ever wants to leave when you do. Once, to get to a church singles dance, I left my car at the Hicksville train station and patriotically rode the fabled Long Island Rail Road to Carle Place and saved a few precious ounces of gas. Nobody at the dance knew when I could get a train back to Hicksville. A young woman had offered to drive me back, so I didn't worry. My easy state of mind lasted about as long as the dance did. Gee-whiz, the would-be driver said, as she primly wrung her hands, she couldn't give me a ride after all, because I was a strange man and her parents wouldn't want her to give potential weirdos rides at one in the morning. She was adamant, and even an offer to let her examine my press card was to no avail. Finally, after considerable waiting and cursing on a chilly train platform, a member of the clean-up crew took me to my car.

Quality does not assure compatibility. This is just a rephrasing of the King Midas Dilemma. Why else would I have gotten intensely bored as the only male in a singles group's post-movie trip to that noted eatery, the Syosset Restaurant? The women—two fairly young, two others better described as "matronly"—were nice enough, but the conversation moved into areas we never explored in Philosophy 200, or even during Freshman Week's beery confessions. Husbands, ex-husbands, baby-sitters, startling propositions and the ultimate truths contained in the movie *Manhattan* made me very, very sleepy. My rather obvious foot-tapping was both a signal for somebody to take me to the parking lot where the group had gathered and a means of combating waves of grogginess.

When opportunity knocks, don't close the door. If you do, try not to catch your fingers in it. This became apparent one Saturday evening at the Lone Star Café, a Fifth Avenue hangout for visiting oilmen, Gucci cowboys and people who crave Pearl Beer and guacamole dip. While waiting at the bar for two other journalists, a young woman—a teacher—began talking to me. Like a light in the control booth at Three Mile Island the word "contact!" began flashing in my mind. We chatted, but when one of the friends I was expecting arrived, I turned my attention to her and felt no allegiance to the teacher whose acquaintance I had just made. After a while the teacher left. This didn't really bother me, because two others had replaced her, and social Nirvana, I was sure, was dawning. As it was, I saw neither of these two again, a state of affairs that made me ruefully appreciate the teacher even as memories of the brief encounter faded. [I can still picture the woman sitting with me at the bar. She might have been a lexicographer. Not for the last time did I miss an opportunity. Where is she now?]

Look for a catharsis. The most effective way of dealing with the feelings of frustration and listlessness that strike everybody at one time or another is to lay them on the table, confront them and then move ahead. Talking with my landlady always helped me. [My landlady in Old Bethpage was a *Newsday* librarian, and I have fond memories of our summer. As I was leaving for a post-internship trip home to Texas, I surprised her with a going away gift, the just-published *Sophie's Choice.*] Once you realize that the great cosmic forces are not thumbing their noses in your direction, the malaise becomes less intense. One Saturday, in a particularly superfluous mood, I walked past a movie line near Greenwich Village. The crowd had just started moving in, and the marquee bore the names of films by Ingmar Bergman, whose work I had never seen.

There followed an evening of Liv Ullmann and rollicking Scandinavian angst. It was just what the doctor ordered. After three hours of *Autumn Sonata* and *Cries and Whispers*, I felt great and practically bounced up to Penn Station.

Courtesy of The Daily Princetonian.

Happy, carefree days as the Sports Features Editor of the Daily Princetonian, 1979.

Chapter 3

Into the New World, or, The Search for the Media Naranja

In the 1980s, I generated a social life from the time-tested ways (introductions, blind luck) and through the personals section of *New York* magazine, with an occasional dip into the *Village Voice* and New York's *Jewish Week.*

Up against the wall, redneck mother? Not quite. A portrait of the writer as a young frozen-food journalist, 1981.

Every week, *New York* offered up columns of possibilities. From the view of twenty-five years later, the process was astoundingly pokey: Find an ad, write a letter, stick in a picture, apply a stamp, mail, and wait. And wait. If a woman responded, the lag time between mail and call could make it hard to remember who was who, so I typically clipped the ad from the magazine and wrote down the date I sent a letter. Occasionally, I noted the name of the woman and when she responded. Until about a decade ago, the technology of romance had changed little since Babylonian singles exchanged cuneiform calling cards at village wells. Introductions were personal, random encounters at parties or on subway platforms, or via cumbersome and thinly informed ads.

Between 1980 and 1987 my relationships resulted from old-fashioned introductions and responses to *New York* and *Village Voice* ads. All involved Jewish women, and all but one lived in Manhattan when we dated. I remember odd details about them. One *New York* ad, which led to an eighteen-month relationship spanning 1985-1986, read, "Witty, Jewish Female Exec—26, seeks Jewish professional, male 26-32, 5'7" or over, who loves NY and wants to share it." One woman had an older father—so old he had fought in the Kaiser's army in World War I. Another's mother escaped on the last children's transport out of Germany. Another tried to win my affections by exclaiming, "I've been fucked so many times I had to get a bigger diaphragm!" One was with me on a cold January night in 1984 when I learned my mother died of cancer in Tyler, Texas. These and other women moved on with their lives—marriage, children, divorces. One died, and two found me on the Internet.

While I was socially asleep during my dozen years of marriage, the Internet blasted apart the technology of the lovelorn.

Online dating has transformed the way people seek, meet, and, sometimes, meet again. It exploded opportunities for browsing and contact, driving curious hearts across multiple time zones in the search for what Chana, from Latin America, called the *media naranja*, a Spanish colloquialism for your "better half" or "significant other." Some sites are general, such as match.com, while others like JDate.com serve a particular religious or ethnic slice. Rightstuffdating.com focuses on graduates of the Ivy League and similar schools. Having lived on my own since October 2002, I hadn't dated since 1987, before technology turned dating into a form of interactive direct marketing. Back in the dating world, I found I liked the online channel's choices and depth of information. Scanning a full profile reveals more facts—along with a surprisingly good sense of a woman's personality—than a half-hour of tortured conversation. As a writer, contacting women online suited my style far better than jostling for attention as just another bald middle-aged guy at a bar or party.

The traditions of my youth, however, were still appealing. In early 2003, I responded to a personals ad in the *Forward* newspaper. Most of the personal ads were geriatric, but one woman in her early forties, Russian, sounded worth a letter. As a writer, I can do nothing if not crank out an attention-grabbing letter. I summoned up my rusty ad-response skills after a fifteen-year hiatus and sent a note to the woman.

A few days later, the phone rang. The Russian, let's call her Nadezhda (the Russian word for hope, which she indeed represented at that time of my life) was calling. My letter worked! She had a very heavy accent, but the talk went well and I got her phone number. I asked her to meet and she agreed. We worked out the details to get together a few days later on Fifth Avenue and Forty-Ninth Street after work.

I remember my excitement at my first real date after the separation and how my teeth chattered. Actually, the dental clicking was a combination of nerves and the bone-snapping cold of the night we met. The temperature must have been in the mid-teens as I scurried out of my office at an accounting firm on Third Avenue around 6:30, dressed in a suit. Despite layers of clothing, the cold seeped into me as if I were in swim trunks. Nadezhda was probably used to just such weather, but my Texas roots still kept me acclimated to balmy Gulf Coast weather.

We had no plans for what to do, where to go. Nadezhda worked in a financial position with a state agency, so that gave us some occupational overlap. I waited on Fifth Avenue at the appointed meeting spot, bouncing from foot to foot to keep the frostbite surely affecting my extremities from spreading.

"Van?" I heard, and turned. I had not seen a picture of Nadezhda, but she knew what I looked like. I saw a well-dressed women with Asiatic features. She reminded me of a Jewish version of the Icelandic singer Björk. As such, she varied greatly from the bred-from-the-*shtetl* variety of Eastern European Jewish women I typically ran with in my single days. For the very first date of my newly single life, I had made a good start. Nadezhda was breathtakingly attractive.

We decided to stroll and find a place to order a drink and warm up. Our search was not random; she made a beeline north to the St. Regis Hotel.

We settled into a booth and I noticed a young Orthodox couple nearby, perhaps in their modest courting mode. They knew how to get to the point of dating.

The waiter brought the drink menu and we ordered glasses of wine. As a total wine neophyte, I seconded her order. The place was relatively quiet, but I strained to understand Nadezhda's Russian accent. We talked about our kids, our work, Russia, the U.S. Every word, every gesture of this first encounter was new to me. After about forty-five minutes Nadezhda excused herself to get the bus back to

Brooklyn, and I had to skitter to Grand Central Terminal for the train to Connecticut. Our first date had reached its conclusion.

I said I would call, and I did. Nadezhda ushered in my new life and I liked her exotic Björk-like appearance and the notion of a social life. I called, I emailed, and I never heard anything back from her.

I never responded to a print-media personal ad again. The first date of my new single life marked the last date generated by my old approach. Within a month, I joined an online dating site. My social life was going digital. The opportunities for searching, finding, chatting and even connecting, I soon learned, were about to increase dramatically.

Dunked in the Digital Dating Pool

I knew about JDate, but I couldn't get myself to join it. I was not yet divorced, and the idea of seriously looking for a new woman felt strange. However, I wanted to do something with my sudden solitude, given my new status as a refugee from a big house to a one-bedroom apartment.

I've always had an affection for off-brand consumer selection. In banking, why would I select Citibank or Manny Hanny when I could go with more daring, maverick options like Amalgamated or European American Bank? My zeal to support the struggling contender extended to dating. At the suggestion of people in MSN's anti-JDate discussion group (yes, it did exist), I signed up with the small but scrappy rival, Jcupid, in February 2003.

On a good night, one hundred women were online at Jcupid. The selection got old fast. Yet what it lacked in quantity it made up for in quality. I met several women there who became, if not lovers, then staunch friends. Plus, the site had technical features that I have yet to see on other dating sites. I especially liked the way it kept track of all emails back and forth with a single woman on the woman's profile page. This feature enabled me to watch the relationship unfurl, like a flower blossoming, as emails zapped back and forth. Other sites simply clump all emails together in sent and received files, so tracking the back and forth with one contact becomes much more difficult. Facebook just adapted this approach to messages, so Jcupid was way ahead of its time (JDate eventually absorbed it).

I can remember the first two women I had contact with quite clearly. I got an email from a French woman in New York, perhaps intrigued by the note on my profile that I was born in France (albeit on the U.S. Air Force base, and we moved back to the U.S. before I was three, so I spoke no French). She sent me a short note, I wrote back, I got her name, checked her out and found she had knocked three years off her age. For the first but no means the last time, I found myself thinking, "She lied to me." Her European style attracted me, but I never could get a date with her.

The second date from Jcupid started at my initiative. I saw a woman who looked like a Jewish Hobbit, even shorter than me, cute enough. I wrote, she wrote, and when she gave me her name, something clicked in my brain. Mora ... short ... had a job in publishing ... then it hit me. I had worked with this Mora at a publishing company in the 1980s. I was an editor at a monthly magazine covering the frozen food industry (I went to Princeton for this? Well, as an editor once told me, "A gig is a gig."); Mora was a secretary and also was my secret office crush (until her boss casually told me he knew all about my mooning over her).

I said nothing to Mora on the phone. I wanted to see her in person to confirm she was the Mora of twenty years earlier. With my impeccable sense of inappropriate planning, I convinced her to meet me at the clock in Grand Central

Terminal. It was March, 2003, the day of the massive anti-war rally in New York, protesting the invasion of Iraq. I figured we could watch the excitement, see the freakiness, have some fun.

We planned to meet on a street corner in the East Fifties, but the huge turnout and stifling crowd control by the NYPD made movement impossible. The sardine-like crowd density made me feel panicked and claustrophobic. I tried calling Mora with my cell phone but I just got her voice mail. She must have been on the subway.

Swaying with the crowd like seaweed at Bikini Bottom, I watched the rally as I fought to reverse directions and reach Grand Central. I saw several people wearing buttons for a politician I had never heard of—someone named "Howard Dean."

Finally I reached Grand Central and found Mora. I was bursting to reveal the big secret. She had not associated my unusual name with her lovestruck coworker of the early Reagan years. Once I saw her, I said, "Mora, it's me, Van. Don't you recognize me? We used to work together. Your boss was Moe, right?"

Gradually, recognition spread over her face. My first great dating coincidence.

We talked about the demonstration, her work after publishing, my life since we last saw each other and all the typical first date/old friends topics. Time had taken its toll on both of us. She wasn't the Yiddish sylph I remembered from twenty years earlier and I didn't see a second meeting in the cards. Or so I thought.

A few months later I attended a Jcupid social event at the bar. I was interested in another woman then, Marsha, a lawyer I had gotten together with twice. I walked upstairs where only a few people had gathered and, to my surprise, saw Marsha and Mora together, chatting away. I smoothed over how I knew the two of them, and maybe told Marsha a few more details. I snapped a picture of them together and for years Marsha used an edited version of that photo on her dating profiles.

So, I chalked that one up to experience. I had many others. I always felt a jolt when I met a new woman and we connected. I would think, "Finally! Normal life, again." Consider what I wrote in my journal late in 2003 about Dulce, a career-changing corporate executive. We both felt a spark and I wrote,

> I finally got to hold hands after 2 ½ wretched years. Woman: Dulce. Place: Compo Beach. Time: around 11 p.m. after our dinner at the Black Duck Café. It felt glorious, her hand warm in, and then on, mine. We held hands, but no foot rubs or anything more intimate. When she dropped me off at my car at the Black Duck, we kissed twice, but not sloppily. Finally! I can still feel phantom warmth and touch on my hand.

We enjoyed cuddle sessions in my creaky 1986 Saab at frigid Connecticut beaches and fervent hand-holding at movies. I printed out her long and affectionate emails, written in bold purple type. "When is your birthday?" she coyly asked one January night, a question that suggests a long time horizon and exotic plans.

She wrote to me:

> Van, I feel like I'm in a strange predicament with you and am not sure how to deal with it. I decided to just tell you honestly what I'm thinking. So, here goes ...
>
> You seem great to me. I mean, great by my

> standards. It is not easy for me to find men that have the special combination of qualities that I appreciate.
>
> That being said, I'm eager to continue getting to know you. However, I have to say honestly that I am disappointed in the way I look right now and don't want you to be disappointed when meeting me. I recently returned to a more healthy lifestyle (exercise and healthful eating) and feel confident that I am now back on the right track.
>
> So, how patient and optimistic are you?

Very patient and optimistic, I assured her. We got along great and she was an assertive PDA/hand-holder at movies and events—I liked that. Then, very quickly, Dulce talked about getting my child together with her nephews, and us coming to her family's Passover seder. I told her I needed to think about that. Result: total silence. She never responded to me again, despite my efforts to restart contact. Her patience must have been limited, I suppose:

> Still nothing from Dulce, although I see she looked at JDate, so she's still alive. I called, emailed, texted, but nothing, so she must be mighty pissed at me.

Five years later, on a date, I saw her in an Indian restaurant. I recognized her instantly and she must have recognized me—I'm the same bald Jewish guy with glasses I was then. But given the circumstances, I decided to keep quiet. I simply noted that Dulce was dining with a man and woman—just the three of them on a Saturday evening.

Too bad about Dulce, but I kept moving. Over five years of on-and-off Internet dating, my batting average hovered around .250, meaning that from about a hundred contacts, twenty to thirty have led to something other than my being ignored, getting a polite thanks-but-no-thanks (or sending the same type of response myself). The others led to an exchange of emails through the dating site or an instant message chat, with a progressively smaller number moving to swaps of personal email addresses, phone calls, and even real meetings—the point, of course, where the contact soars or crashes. It took about ninety seconds to tell whether any chemistry existed; the process was probably the same on the distaff side. After two minutes we were either starry-eyed or checking our watches. To be honest, we could both tell; only in a few cases did one of us wildly misjudge the situation.

I figure I sent about 3,000 emails on JDate and got 2,000 back. Of course, a smaller group of women generated all that traffic—one woman might generate dozens of emails back and forth over years. Match and Jcupid account for another 1,000. That's a lot of trying, blind alleys, long distance faux-romances, digital heartbreak, self-delusion and self-acceptance. And some of them actually led to something.

I felt plenty of exasperation and frustration. At one low point, I wrote,

> I believe I'm making an emotional breakthrough today. I scurried to Barnes & Noble to flip through self-help books as essay research and I quickly found Dr. Laura Schlessinger's *Ten Stupid Things Men Do*. The first stupid thing—"Stupid Chivalry." That hit me like a lightning bolt. That's me, accepting all kinds of nonsense from [name redacted], excusing her, hoping she'll change, taking enormous emotional damage in my longing for her, although plenty of circumstances warn me that it would never work.
>
> So, as my mind churned through these matters

> today, I realized in the words of the *Alfie* theme song, "What's it all about?" Really—I've been pursuing online romance for four years, since Jcupid in February 2003. What do I have to show for it? How close am I—have I ever come close—to my ultimate goal? Am I serious about finding romance, warmth, somebody to share some aspects of my life? Am I spending too much time in a fruitless wheel-spinning quest, a scavenger hunt for inappropriate women? Isn't it time I stopped jacking around, being the nectar-sipping hummingbird, and really found a flower?"

The nectar could be emotionally addictive. I over-scrutinized profiles for revisions that then rubbed my self-doubts and insecurities raw. I mused:

> I noted she updated her profile yesterday with a new screen name; perhaps the old one was too obscure. I noted also she's seeking somebody with a doctorate, nothing less. Her profile also referred to time in bed, which made my chest lurch. Obviously that's on her mind.

But hope was always springing eternal on JDate and Match. The opportunities endlessly beckoned, floating in the digital ether then usually drifting away. So:

> A bunch of promising JDate contacts came up like snake eyes. One is in Merrick, NY, so that's not good geography. Another wrote to me, a NYC executive, 5' 8", the last in the world I expected to like my profile enough to write. I wrote, she read, nothing, I wrote again yesterday, "Come on, my

> Sweet, don't stop now." Her screen name is Sweet, or some form of it. Then I chatted with a woman who looked at me. She launched a barrage of questions that I answered, bemoaned the "nightmare" of JDate and the boorish behavior of men. Twice she said she didn't think we were a match, and she wrote she didn't think I was attracted to strong women. All this happened while I was watching *24*, too—Jack Bauer tangles with his father and brother. She came across as cold and suspicious; dare I say unfeminine? For a woman who's had awful experiences, she did her best to alienate me. Yet she didn't seem to want to end the chat. She sounded like a horror. Abrupt, lacking any of the coquette. Never married—I can see why.

Online dating from this point on became a numbers game, a slow, halting, confusing process. I didn't know what to expect, I didn't limit myself to searching just in my area. I hesitated at first, but got into the swing of contacting women and, in some cases, getting contacted. I couldn't believe a woman would ignore me when we seemed to be such a good initial match, but I learned that's the way the world works, that I should not even expect an acknowledgment. I described online dating as a social version of the Rubik's Cube. All the parts are turning, and at any one time you can see only a few of them. While I was dispatching my heartfelt notes, others did the same, and I could only try and hope. Most were ignored; of course, I also sent plenty of thanks-but-no-thanks notes to women—but I always responded. I gave them credit for reaching out, and these women merited at least an acknowledgment. Some were gracious:

> I do have to tell you one thing, just so you

> know... I actually just started dating someone from town here. The whole crazy thing was he found me on JDate exactly the same time you did—but I keep running into him for bagels. It's been very pleasant as he's basically down the street! We have no idea if it will amount to anything ... but I'm a lousy multiple-dater!
>
> I'd love to keep getting to know you as a friend if you're comfortable with that .... I really truly enjoyed your company, and often have friends who are looking to meet somebody. So I just wanted to throw that out to you and see how you felt about it.

Receiving a positive response merely started the process. The exchange of real-world contact details, the IMs, the phone calls followed. And even then, surprises inevitably lurked. Consider my encounter with a woman I'll call Spacey Stacy. We set a 7 p.m. rendezvous on the Upper West Side of Manhattan. The vibe turned strange that afternoon, as I walked to the train station near my apartment. She called my cell phone to nail down the details, then said she'd had "a rough day" and "too many margaritas" the night before (Halloween). Finally she said we could get coffee "and if it worked out, maybe dinner." The words and tone rang alarm bells, but I shrugged them off.

I arrived first at the appointed Starbucks and grabbed a table. I recognized Stacy when she came in—hair a little shorter than in her picture, but the same cute pug nose. She sat down and abruptly asked about a grueling work project I had endured that week. We complimented each other on how closely we resembled our profile photos. We talked about her job search and smiled through strained silences. I offered to get some drinks. She waved me off. "Just get one for yourself."

"Do you want to go someplace else?" I asked.

"No."

After I returned with my Tazo iced tea, we spoke about her relations with her ex, her dancing classes, get-to-know-you stuff. Finally Stacy declared, "I don't sense this is a love connection, so I'm going to go. Good luck with your search."

I was stupefied. We had been together fifteen minutes, if that. "Okay, then. I guess I'll talk to you later," I muttered. That sounded moronic. "No, I guess I won't be talking to you later." Stacy strode into the New York night, leaving me speechless. Finally, I took the dregs of tea and hit Broadway, now swarming with happy couples touching, strolling, snacking, laughing—or so my eyes told me. On this night, I was not among them.

From the churning mass of possibilities, contacts emerged in thematic waves. There were the Latina therapists, the little white liars (regarding age, location, number of kids, Clinton-era photos), and the creative collective of designers, P.R. mavens, teachers, writers, and even rabbis. I surfed the Princeton wave, meeting and sometimes dating women whose son, brother, or cousin graduated—also a few Princetonians. The Tiger connection on my profile definitely attracted attention—no coy "Ivy League graduate" description for me.

Over the years I learned how online contacts can swell quickly into rainbow-colored intensity, enveloping a man and woman in a virtual intimacy of nightly gossip and revelation. But like a soap bubble, what feels like the start of a real friendship or even romance can pop and vanish, leaving only a filmy residue in memory. A woman I'll call Motek, for example, called me "very special" during one of our lengthy conversations and emailed photos of her kids. I was ready to drive hundreds of miles to meet her, out of surging curiosity (although I delayed this obvious next step because I worried my rattletrap car couldn't handle the trip. Stupid me). Then

Motek avoided my contacts. She never explained why, but the friendship tanked immediately after I called her cell phone while she was at dinner with a man she termed the "competition." More on that later.

Ninety-seven percent of the contacts went nowhere. One percent, at most, went somewhere exciting. And in two percent, warmth and affection took root as two people groped for common ground in the space between romance and indifference. These friendships settled into easy patterns once we realized they would never be anything else.

Sometimes the relationship bounced between longing and loathing, attraction and repulsion based on forces unseen. Chana and I were in contact on-and-off for years. We kept in touch despite hurt feelings, misunderstandings, and bouts of online hide-and-go-seek. Finally settling into a comfortable rhythm, I called her *mi brujita*, "my little witch," because of the spell she cast on me, and she teased me about my "cyber-*novias*," or online sweethearts. And then we met, felt nothing and ended our contacts permanently.

That's the way online dating goes. Something works great up to a point, and then you discover that outside of being Jewish and speaking English, you are simply two strangers with nothing to share and nowhere to go.

In some cases, however, we found a groove and remain platonic contacts with technology serving as the useful go-between. We talk, we IM, and sometimes we get together to catch up on life. I reached the point where I didn't presume to know a woman based on our contact on dating sites. I've been in touch with at least a dozen women who have moved beyond online dating into co-habitation, engagement, and (*mazel tov!*) marriage. Through all the stages, we've been able to sustain a simple friendship with each other.

Thanks, Facebook.

Chapter 4

Date Me, I'm From Texas, or, The Master of the Good Screen Name

Astute marketers know the value of a good name, one that captures an essence, provokes thought, and closes the sale. Over my years of online dating, I took that approach. I'm a writer, I freelanced for *Advertising Age*, and I know the value of a clear message. And what is online dating, other than the direct marketing of a single product (i.e., me, Me, ME)? To effectively brand myself, I needed cute pictures, a compelling profile, and a snappy screen name. With a unique selling proposition, I could tilt the odds in my favor in that split-second when a woman decides whether to respond to an email—or ignore me.

Upon joining Jcupid, I tinkered with names like Van, VW, and even Tazio, the Italian middle name I loathed as a kid but came to grudgingly like as an adult because it is so freakishly different and "ethnic." (My father, obsessed with race cars, named me after the Italian race car driver Tazio Nuvolari.) But everything I chose seemed either boring or bizarre. I got closer to the mark with Ze'ev, a Hebrew name that sounds like Van and that I use at religious services. Ze'ev worked well enough to remain the name on one profile; it drew women who thought I was Israeli. Still, Ze'ev lacked a certain Van-ness and emotional resonance.

So I doodled possibilities reflecting my upbringing

amidst the balmy breezes and pastoral landscapes of the Rio Grande Valley—Mission, Texas, to be exact, Home of the Grapefruit and Tom Landry, first coach of the Dallas Cowboys. Some ideas:

ValleyGuy. Too obscure, and the U.S. has lots of Valleys, including San Fernando, Red River, and Death.

TexDude. Sounds lame, and I never think of myself as a "dude."

Missionary. This cleverly alludes to my hometown, but it could excessively appeal to Southern Baptists. Also, people might assume Missionary implies a limited erotic repertoire. Come to think of it, that assumption might also get Baptists knocking on my digital door.

Then, clawing up from the overactive self-marketing node in my brain, there emerged "TexasHoldEm." The more I noodled, the better it sounded. Free associations clustered around it like lobbyists at the Texas Railroad Commission. It tells a short story in four syllables. Soon, TexasHoldEm became the screen name that I used on three sites.

South Conway Avenue, Mission, on the "other side" of the railroad tracks.

You might ask, why make a big deal out of my Texas provenance? I left Texas for Princeton in 1976 and haven't lived in that state since the summer of 1977. My returns for high school reunions and family visits are rare. I've lived in New York and Connecticut far longer than I lived in Texas. And yet, those early years are forever imprinted on me, through education, values, memories, even my way of talking (I joke that after a few Coronas I sound just like LBJ).

I've made my peace with that influence—and I've discovered that Lone Star roots are a great marketing tactic, endlessly provocative at cocktail parties and singles sites. I could always spin tales of guns, black-helicopter obsessives, the Dallas Cowboys, the cultural disputations of the high school cultures known as the "ropers and the dopers," the complex relations of Anglos and Hispanics and the dangerous allure of Mexico, located about four miles down Conway Avenue and across from Anzalduas Park, on the other side of the Rio Grande. One of my favorite stories involves a conversation I overheard between two local worthies in the summer of 1976, after I had graduated from Mission High School. Let's call them Waylon and Willie. As I wrote on June 19, 1976 (names and expletives deleted):

> "How's Boystown these days?" Willie asked [referring to the red-light district in Reynosa, across the Rio Grande from McAllen].
>
> Waylon said the action was "Okay."
>
> Willie took something of a dim view of the area, but Waylon sounded quite enthusiastic. "Wow! One of the places really has a nice atmosphere with columns, plants, chandeliers," he informed us.
>
> "Sounds more like a bank," I said.
>
> "Well, if you want a piece of ass you can get it

> cheaper (and cleaner) here, but I go for the atmosphere," Waylon said.
>
> "Once," he added, "I found one who knew my older brother real well."
>
> "When I first moved down here," Willie said, "I'd go down there and stay for hours just talking to the girls and looking at the places."
>
> They broached the subject of Nuevo Laredo whorehouses: "Well some guys tell me, 'Them Laredo whores is the best around,' " Willie joked in a mock thick Texas accent. "And I tell them, 'Well, hell, I'm going there this afternoon, so I'll be sure to check 'em out.' "
>
> "You'd be surprised at what goes on in this town," Waylon told me.
>
> I can imagine.

Reflecting those roots, I note in one profile, "I practice an archaic Southern chivalry: I hold open doors, stand up when a lady enters the room, write thank-you notes, and help her take her coat off."

My profiles carried a teasing line, "Now, who can guess the multiple meanings of my screen name?" That shameless come-on indeed attracted women to my fiesta of verbal playfulness. The name and line invited women to casually contact me. A woman I'll call BruchaFromBoca wrote the most memorable response. Her jaw-dropping first email, in its entirety, read, "Masturbation comes to mind, but far be it from this lady of Boca to admit to it ..."

To which I quickly replied, "Very good! Obviously we think along the same lines. I was picturing holding somebody else (TexasHoldEm, after all, not TexasHoldIt), but you've certainly got the right idea. Now, the other meanings: I really am from Texas originally, so there's that connotation.

TexasHoldEm is a form of poker, and card-playing was very popular in my family when I was young—my mother enjoyed nothing better than playing poker late into the night with her aunts during family vacations to San Antonio."

Photos on my profile gave visual clues to the meanings, some obvious, others indecipherable without explanation. One photo heavy with Texas atmosphere showed me at a Houston shooting range blasting away at targets with a Glock pistol. I told women that I was "getting in touch with my inner NRA." In another, I clutched two squirming Yorkshire Terrier puppies to my chest, with the caption, "Holdin' 'Em." In a picture from a high school reunion, I'm grinning impishly as I sit next to a hugely pregnant classmate from Mission; she points one finger at her stomach and another at me (dream on).

I hoped my pitch would attract women, but I also was drawn to women who used TX in their screen names. One friend, TexDG, says that the name generated curiosity from men. She wrote to me, "Guys from the east coast think Texas is 'exotic.' " Many figure she supported Bush in the election; as she said, "They think the whole state voted for George—yes, a bunch a yahoos us'ns."

"Did you get into any heated discussions? Could they get past their notions of Exotic Laurie to who you really are?" I asked.

"No heated discussions. I just don't go there. LOL—funny about that," she wrote back. "A lot of the guys just want to know what color my undies are!"

Another woman, GoodListenerTX, commented, "I have received more emails with this name than either my first screen name of honestmom or afierytopaz. Most people couldn't spell fiery let alone grasp the meaning of topaz. (I know it is an obscure fact that topaz comes in colors other than blue.) I would have been a ruby but it was too cliché."

These are women in Texas; plenty of men and women in the state throw TX onto their screen names. My all-time favorite was Texasbabydoll—who could resist *that* image? The contacts get even more interesting when folks (like me) fly the Texas identity like a battle flag when they live out of state. I particularly like the profile of JudyTX, a woman I actually met outside of dating sites because of our maverick political interests. Her profile said, "I am a proud native Texan, currently a Manhattanite (lots more Jews here—including family—but the sunsets are smaller)."

You'll notice a pattern here. TexDG, GoodListenerTX and another called TexanAtHeart all responded to me, and women from the South and Latin America also have the fine grace to pen a polite reply. Some declined further contact, pointing to the distance between us, and I understood their concerns. Others, however, have become enduring friends. Whatever the future holds—as friends or strangers whose yearnings touched for an instant—I can say to all of them *zol zein mit mazel*, Yiddish for "you should be with luck."

TexDG and I still have playful conversations that sound like two friends yakking over coffee. Once, we were dishing about women's profile pictures. She wrote, "Jewish girls wear bikinis?"

I replied, "Sure, Jewish women in bikinis and low-cut tops. I'm amazed at some of the photos—stretched out on fur rugs, sprawled across a bed, in a bikini with *the kids* in the picture."

The Texas and Jewish sides merged with one of my very first contacts on Jcupid. A woman in northern Mexico wrote to me. She posted no photo on her profile and didn't indicate why she was on a Jewish website. I asked about her background, and she replied,

> why am I interested in a jewish site? is because I have jewish roots, but nobody in my family practice judaism. In this area where I live u can't find jewish

people, and I'm not interested in meeting more non-jewish guys.

Given my future contacts with women in Latin America and trips to see them, this short-lived connection touched on some key interests—dare I say obsessions?—in my life. Indeed, I often wondered if any of my high school heartthrobs might be distantly Jewish, descendants of *conversos* or *marranos* hounded out of Spain and Portugal to settle and live secretly, in fear of the Inquisition, in Mexico and then Texas. Could any of them be the elusive JAP—Jewish Aztec Princess—integrating my Texas and Jewish elements? Did their grandmothers light candles on Friday, did their families avoid pork and cover mirrors after the death of a relative? I never found any evidence of this, but I like the great guessing game. As that email from Mexico indicated, the JAPs are out there. Call it wishful thinking, but some Valley friends definitely give me a Jewish Aztec Princess vibe.

At the Los Ebanos ferry to Mexico. The people behind Operation Fast & Furious must have missed the message.

More typically, I met Texas Jews in New York. I could always sniff them out using "texdar," my variation on the concept of "gaydar." Like their counterparts back home, these urban cowgirls almost always replied to me and we sometimes met. We had great conversations about hometowns, educations, and bloodlines. One woman even had family members named Michelson, as I do, so we are probably related from way back in the 1860s, when the first Michelsons bid a not-so-fond *auf wiedersehen* to Germany and headed for post-Confederacy Texas.

> Where the heck in Hidalgo County did you grow up? I'm from Dallas. We should compare our Jewish genealogical roots.

The Texas identity does carry risks. One on one, women were curious about the place and kept any prejudices in check, but in public somebody always felt compelled to spout off. I once attended a Friday night singles event where a Chabad rabbi (!) said, "Oh, you're the guy from that hick town!" On a singles hiking event in Connecticut, I was trapped in a car with people who assured me that Republicans would never go on a hike because they hate the environment. Later, a man said, "You're from Texas, so you must really hate Bush."

I thought, What a *pinche pendejo cabron* ("dumbass" and even more insulting meanings), as we used to say in Hidalgo County. To this perfect specimen of BDS (Bush Derangement Syndrome), I replied, "I like what President Bush says and does, and I definitely approve of the War on Terror." That shut him up pronto.

I was ready to talk when women asked about Texas. My whole brand positioning depended on delivering the goods bout that unique upbringing. Without some colorful anecdotes and family stories, I'd get an "all hat, no cattle" reputation. Fortunately, I remember (or wrote down) *everything*. What follows are some of my favorite informational crunchies:

- My family has been in Texas for a long, long time. There are little kids down there that are seventh-generation Texans. My great-great-grandfather, Chayim Schwarz, was the first ordained rabbi in Texas. In 1873 he moved to Hempstead from Germany. He's the guy on the cover of the book, *Jewish Stars in Texas: Rabbis and Their Work*, by Hollace Ava Weiner.

Mission's historic Border Theater, our very own last picture show palace.

- I graduated from the same high school that my mother did, exactly forty years later. Talk about continuity.

- When I was a kid, the family story I heard was that relatives passed through San Antonio in the 1870s and they could still see blood on the walls of the Alamo. The spookiest Texas stories always involve the Alamo.

- Texas breeds wacky politics. I had a high school typing teacher who argued that motorcycle-helmet laws were a form of communism. At my tenth reunion in 1986, a classmate was certain that the Sandinistas were going to march up from Nicaragua and invade Harlingen. The wife of another friend used to talk earnestly about "the black helicopters."

- Growing up in Texas and then moving to the Northeast scrambled my politics. People down there think I'm a commie-hippie-pinko-treehugger. Folks in the Northeast think I'm a crypto-fascist Texas gun nut. The truth is actually in the middle. I'm a free thinker, and that drives people crazy.

- Heard of Kinky Friedman? Heck, I interviewed Ol' Kinky once for a magazine article I wrote about the Lone Star Roadhouse in New York. We had a real nice visit, too.

- A college roommate thought my mother sounded exactly like Lady Bird Johnson.

- You find six streams of political philosophy in Texas: Liberal, Moderate, Conservative, Extremely Conservative, and East Texas.

The longer I did online dating, the more I found my profile worked exactly as I wanted it to. Years of tinkering polished it to a high gloss of effective communications. I mentioned *The Odyssey* and the final lines of *Ulysses* by James Joyce ("and his heart was going like mad and yes I said yes I will Yes."); I spoke frankly about my interest in Judaism. I skipped, to the greatest extent possible, the clichés of dating profiles: fine wine, walks on the beach, skiing, and whatever I figured the other guys—those tall, dark, rich and handsome swordsmen I imagined running wild—were saying. I couldn't compete except on my own terms, and I made a joke about that. So I accentuated the positives that would work for women who would want a guy like me.

Walks on the beach? How about a picnic and a walk around the lake?

I eventually evolved away from the screen name that worked so well. TexasHoldEm got stale after a while. Even a good name needs a refresher. Nice new merchandise always gets at least a glance from the window shoppers, so my last iteration at JDate used the name OurYidinHavana, chosen after I went on a week-long Jewish humanitarian trip to Cuba. I liked the ring of it, the reference to the Graham Greene novel *Our Man in Havana* and the exotic locale of the trip. Here's a compilation of my evolving profiles:

> Like Odysseus, I am a man of twists and turns, sometimes blown off course but always eager to continue the journey. My path has taken me from Mission, a small town in South Texas (only Jewish family there) to Princeton, Brooklyn, and now Connecticut. I'm a little different from what you may have encountered before, a mix of the border and the city, Southwest and Northeast. Through trial and error I have found a satisfying place in life. I live in hope, not fear, and I'll be a loyal friend, witty chat pal, and overall mensch. I have a strong Jewish identity, and I strive to live an ethical life. The writings of Rabbis Abraham Twerski and Arye Kaplan have deeply influenced me. I enjoy languages, and have studied Hebrew, Yiddish, Spanish, Russian, and, most recently, Portuguese; I don't claim to speak any of them but just the act of studying opens new worlds and words for me and keeps my middle-aged brain challenged. I just need somebody to practice with. I have eclectic music tastes, from Latin (Cuba's Los Van Van is a favorite) to Cajun to hard-core honky-tonk to smooch-jazz to bossa nova. I practice an archaic Southern chivalry; I hold open doors, stand up when a lady enters the room, write thank-you notes, and help you get your coat off. If you're seeking the oh-so-elusive tall single straight Jewish male, I score high on every attribute except "tall." (And four out of five ain't bad, is it?).

A great relationship would be warm, honest, surprising, open to disagreements but never in a spiteful way, considerate, and understanding. A man and a woman connect on mental, emotional and, of course, physical levels. Hugs, kisses, Cool Whip, you know what I mean. And moderation in all things, including moderation.

The woman I find will probably be an artist, writer, PR maven, teacher, psychologist, or consultant with a good head on her pretty shoulders, who appreciates experiences more than material goods. She's had her dalliances with bad boys, boozers, abusers, psychos and anti-Semites and can appreciate a man who treats her with respect and can provide buckets of affection and imagination. Such a woman is inventive, fun, creative, involved in Judaism, takes good care of herself and, most of all, LIKES herself. I love kids and am sensitive to issues of custody and visitation; if we click, I will put heart and soul into making the relationship work, however complex our lives. Just try me. Since I once worked in the accounting industry, please comply with GAAP regulations (Genuinely Adorable in Appearance and Personality).

Where will we go for the perfect first date? I'm open to anything: a synagogue event, a diner, an encounter group (yes, that's happened), a quiet setting where we can talk and see what we're about. Magic requires nothing more complex. After that, heaven knows, anything goes.

Chapter 5

What I Liked and What They Said

The constant wordsmithing of my profiles paid dividends in contacts. The messaging always got high marks for literary value. The responses to Judaism surprised me, in that some women thought I was "too religious" for them, although I don't keep kosher and, at the time I was active, didn't belong to a synagogue. I kept informed on Jewish issues, strongly supported Israel and attended pro-Israel rallies whenever crises brought mass events to the United Nations Plaza. But for the women that mattered, the upfront Judaism sent a clear signal of how we could connect. And I enjoyed my share of contacts from women who weren't going to sit back and miss out on their chance at a good thing.

One intro email says:

Dear Tex:

I've always liked bald men. (My three favorite people in the world were/are bald: my brother, my father, my grandfather). But what I really like are smart men. On a par with that are kind men. That you like the arts and culture, even better. And best, you seem to like helping others. And (does it get any better?) you're Jewish too!

I love your photos. You've inspired me to put

> some of my nature shots up on my profile. You sound like a life-long learner. Me too. What are currently writing about? I'm studying in a helping profession (my contribution to *tikkun olam*) [a Hebrew term that means "repair the world"]. I also perform classical music.
>
> Sorry this is a bit disjointed. I've read too many profiles today, but yours is a stand out. Hope you will look mine over and respond.
>
> P.S. What a romantic quote. Is it James Joyce?

Being straight about my interest in Judaism also connected me to a very specific dating cohort: women rabbis. Some were full-time pulpit rabbis, while others combined their rabbinic background with another career, such as therapy or social work. Whatever the background, we always had plenty to talk about.

One rabbi—now happily married—gave me a *tefillin* set (defined earlier as black straps with black boxes containing Bible verses that Jews wear during morning services on weekdays) that I use when I attend the Sunday morning *minyan* at my synagogue. I let her know I how touched I was by the gift and I use it and always think of her.

Another observation: women rabbis always host excellent seders. I know from experience. They're rabbis! They're women! Would you expect anything less?

The only downside to dating a rabbi—when you go with her to a Jewish event she'll typically get sidetracked talking to a colleague, leaving you to your own devices for a quarter-hour or more. I know from experience.

When women and I connected through Judaism, we often shared other interests. A passion for faith translated into connections involving creativity, languages and social issues.

For example, K in Connecticut, a slender, athletic redhead and educator, wrote me:

> I don't know if you will get this email since you are not a paying member. We chatted the other night. I wished you *Spaconi Nochi* [goodnight in Russian]. I love that you speak Russian and that you have such a strong Jewish identity. I also love the literary in you and your kind smile. We have many common interests. You seem chivalrous and just the sort of person who has the passion for life that I am looking for. You aren't afraid to show yourself and be involved in your Judaism. I would look forward to chatting more with you.

K and I dated several times and I thought highly of her. I still fondly remember our first date at a Thai restaurant in New Haven. I escorted her back to her car in a parking garage late at night, which she appreciated. No romance happened. She wanted a man without young children, and she found what she wanted. I met her husband at a party that they held before moving to another region. She still sends me updates on her life there and I've given her job leads.

What drew me to a profile? I always liked women who were educated and articulate. But being blessed with XY chromosomes, I'm as visual as the next guy. Photos first grabbed my attention. A woman could write random ALL-CAPS gibberish ... with mindless ... ellipses ... and text talk LOL ROFLMA ((((hugs))))) OMG smiley face, but with attractive photos, she'll still get rapt attention from guys who grow dizzy with desire at the sight of a well-turned ankle. That included me. Guys want to gobble the eye candy before they glance at the radishes and rutabaga.

No photo generally meant bad news in the appearance department, although I was always willing to accommodate women who, for work reasons, didn't want their photos online. These were the therapists, social workers and criminal defense attorneys. Otherwise, I had an innate ability to pick out profiles of Russians, Iranians and Latinas everywhere; it must have been the dramatic eye makeup and Slavic/Hispanic pouts (recall that my first post-marriage date was with the perfectly packaged Nadezhda). Just about every woman I ever wrote to with those backgrounds responded to me, and vice versa. Women from Israel, while great looking, never really connected, unless they were Americans who had moved there.

I often liked the pictures and never contacted the women. I appreciate a snug sundress or evening gown as much as the next guy, but I can tell when I have zero chance of a response. And if a profile clearly indicated I wouldn't make the grade (height, location, career, kid issues) then I wouldn't write. But I could enjoy a stroll through the candy shop. However, I found hundreds of women worth a contact; beyond the photos, what appealed to me? Here is a fanciful best-of profile that pulls together all themes I liked, mixed with a dollop of wishful thinking:

> I am looking for a smart, creative man who is passionate about life and see the humor (and the irony) in what we experience each day. Please don't send a tease or a flirt—be a big boy and think for yourself.
>
> The combination of chemistry and compatibility—a mix of friendship, affection, love, and sexual passion—is what I seek. Compassion and strength of character resonate with me, along with warmth, integrity and sincerity. I yearn for a big,

open heart and a big, open mind in a worldly man who is generous in spirit and with his emotions. A touch of vulnerability can be sexy.

What about me? Red hair, pale skin, I glow in the dark. My favorite novelists include Anita Shreve and Alan Furst. I'm an interesting combination of warm, eccentric and worldly with a liberal sprinkling of Mother Earth. I am a thinking man's woman, part angel, part devil. My angel is intelligent, decent, loving, romantic warm and caring. She is classy, feminine, understanding and a giving friend (no, she is not a dog). My devil is brainy, ironical, hot, loves to laugh and can't stand boredom. I enjoy hiking, live music and being with interesting creative types who remind me that my gray matter matters. For movies, I like indie foreign or classics with good scripts and interesting characters ... Shabbat candles are lit weekly and I am committed to living a Jewish life, including being in touch with my spirituality, growing through learning, doing mitzvoth and giving back to the community. I like to reserve my shabbat afternoons for private times with my special somebody.

I can dress just right for a day at the beach, an evening at the opera and especially for midnight with you. I enjoy being a woman and I could give Joan Holloway on *Mad Men* a run for the money. You'll find toe-cleavage shoes in my closet, just be warned.

On our first date, we'll know we have something special when the conversation suddenly leads to a meeting of the eyes in recognition that you can talk to me, and I to you, the way you really are and think.

> The relationship I want would involve spending weekends and holidays and certainly Jewish holidays/Friday evenings together and paying lots of attention to each other. We would have a relationship that's a harbor from the world's troubles. There should be mutual admiration and trust, and acceptance and understanding of each other's strengths and weaknesses. We would create a peaceful, welcoming home full of children and guests. We'd laugh, walk, eat and spend quality time together in bed. And not just napping, either.

Notable emails sent to me:

> You do indeed sound interesting, creative and enlightened—and I know there aren't that many of you out there; however, your face bears a resemblance to my ex's and that's something I cannot feel comfortable with at this juncture in my post divorcehood.

> Thanks for your compliments. If truth be known, I'm actually 62, and MUCH too old for you. I wish you lots of luck, though, in your search.

> Thanks for taking my comments about the child support seriously, it does mean a lot to me as a measurement of the man.

> HAHAHAHAH I LOVE YOU SO MUCH! I WANT TO MEET YOU. I feel running my heart because of you, you are guilty.

> Hi Van/Ze'ev. You were very candid in your

> profile and in our email conversation the other night so I thought I'd tell you a bit more about myself—this time without the generous handholding and comforting anonymity offered by our Cyrano the Reading Specialist [the woman writing this email was looking at men with a friend who actually had a profile, hence the literary reference to a go-between] ... Like you, I like to read and write, am interested in matters of spirit, strive to behave ethically and with compassion, and enjoy literature, philosophy, the arts and Jewish thought, symbolism, custom and culture. I am blessed with wonderful friends—most of them, at the moment, women. I noticed that some people's profiles focused on what they like to do (doesn't everybody like watching the sun set, having candlelit dinners and taking long walks on the beach?), what kinds of clothes they like to wear, or what kind of bodies they have. And then they list the hobbies, fashion sense and body types they require of their prospective mates. I liked your profile because, like the one I intend to write if I ever get to that stage, it seemed to offer a peek at your essence rather than your shell ....

For the record, simplicity and a winning smile can be enough to lead to a great connection. My Significant Other simply said this on her profile:

> I am honest, stable, creative, nice, a loyal friend, plus a good listener. I love to go to the movies, listen to music (singer/songwriters), go to a museum, walk, and am looking forward to having more time for travel.

And you know what? What she says in her profile is exactly what we do and share. It was as simple as that.

Chapter 6

The Functional Value of Heartbreak, or, Vendetta and the Swan

Much as in a job interview, the stories we tell on dates are designed to make good first impressions. In fact, so much of this adult dating stuff seemed like nothing more than the recitation of preset narratives. Two people become acquainted and, as they proceed, start talking. Initially, conversations rarely progress beyond the standard questions posed and reliable answers proffered. If the elusive chemistry exists, the masks slip down and less polished selves may emerge. Then the real connection begins.

That "real connection" happened very few times in my online dating journey. We clicked and I could sense potential, the first rustling of distilled hope and longing against a background of increasingly mechanical introductions. A woman and I would talk and share, or, if we lived close enough (not always the case), actually meet and stroll through the city or a park. We would reveal jagged bits of biography to signal trust, a willingness to explore what our contact could become. Those bits, I discovered, could also be a warning: beware.

I recall one lingering summer afternoon picnic on a lake with a woman I'll call the Swan. After stop-and-go contacts, the warmth of the encounter convinced me that we both had our hearts pointed in the same direction. To my shock, she leaned over and kissed me and I finally got the message. But later, standing in the parking lot, the Swan remarked, "I could bolt at any time." I remembered but ignored this comment, so laden with prophecy.

And bolt she did. Call it a matter of timing, of circumstance, of appearance, or simply, "She's just not that into you." The exact recipe of the fatal brew does not matter; I've always thought that if there's a will, there's a way, and for one of us the will was not there. Our fitful migrations into each other's lives left me feeling buoyant and then, always, bereft and abandoned. Similar possibilities flickered and ended—throttled by distance, hesitation, self-delusion, misunderstandings, the competition. I sketch some of those stories elsewhere. I had my share of stunned surprises staring at the final email, the last blunt conversation, the ceiling at midnight. And I caused my own share of disappointment and confusion.

Yet I found that heartbreak carries a functional value. I've hung around management consultants enough in my career to adapt their world view. I sometimes think in terms of costs and benefits, the bottom line, the so-what learned from a situation, moving from the current state to a future state. Could I ever find the ultimate MECE relationship, that is, "mutually exclusive and collectively exhaustive"? (MECE is a grouping principle that management consultants use to find solutions to client problems. Come to think of it, a durable relationship should, in fact, be mutually exclusive and collectively exhaustive, don't you think?) Never one to know when to hold 'em and when to fold 'em, I would construct a flow chart of romance through project-management milestones, digressions, decision trees and quantitative analyses. That net-net value of heartbreak and experience emerged in response to questions that singles like to ask. Over the years, my dates were curious about what had worked and failed, my online experiences, my emotional engagement, what I was seeking. Did I date much? Did anything click?

Such questions are more than light banter at Starbucks. While I was once memorably called a "self-involved prick who just doesn't get it," I actually do have some basic insights into the dynamics of dating and the human condition. These kinds of questions are anything but casual time-killers; I've read enough Deborah Tannen books to know about rapport talk and the urge to connect. They aim to sound out my past and intentions, my goals, my hopes, my wariness and openness. After initial hesitation to talk about the past, I learned to combine honesty and discretion. When asked, I replied, "Yes, I had some things that looked promising. We really connected. But the timing wasn't right. They just didn't work out."

But life went on in its maddening, hope-surging way. As I started chasing the Swan, I contacted Vendetta, a woman whose online disappointments and world-weary bitterness created a space that I thought I could fill as the decent normal guy—not tall, not rich, having no ski chalet, but not too colossal of a shmuck, either. She asked me about my JDate experiences and I remarked I would be meeting somebody interesting in a few days (the Swan). Vendetta replied,

> If nothing works out with the woman you are meeting this week, or the ones you are currently in touch with, let's make a time to meet. One of the things that's happened w/me on JDate recurrently is that I make a time a couple of weeks out to meet someone, and in the meantime they meet someone else, or their childhood sweetheart moves back to town, or their borderline daughter is cutting herself too much for them to meet someone, or they've decided they needed a taller woman (I get this too),

> etc, etc. So, I've learned that it is better to make a time to meet sooner, and limit the online fantasy life that builds.

We kept swapping warm emails and I indeed wanted to meet Vendetta, to keep my emotional investment portfolio diversified. Using email only, Vendetta and I worked out a meeting plan. She never wanted to talk on the phone, an oddity that concerned me, but I told myself it was part of her off-beat charm and obvious intelligence. Educated and caring, she looked so perky with her auburn hair and Semitic features that I tolerated the nonsense just to meet her in person (you know how guys are). The first time we ever spoke was the day I took vacation time from work to travel to her city for lunch at a restaurant where she and her ex ate—she'd slipped in that detail. I liked both her smarts and appearance, and could see meeting again. She had some quirks—such as the bias against phone calls—but I could accept them. I felt good on the trip home.

Once I got back, Vendetta turned a full-throttle chainsaw on my musings when she wrote:

> What I am realizing is that I am so far away from having much settled with the divorce that I don't think it makes sense for me to even think I can date someone out of town at this point. It's too much to imagine that I could relocate, given all the custody stuff—I think I was being somewhat hopeful but unrealistic. As I thought, [name redacted] is starting the "I'm taking you to court" in earnest now, as he had threatened .... I think I'm in too much flux to even pursue something in town, much less a few hours away.
>
> Still, I really enjoyed your company and hope

> we can in some way remain connected. I would understand if you have other priorities in your life that would make that not an interesting option. But I love writing to you, and it would be nice to have another smart, compassionate friend in the world.
>
> Let me know what you think.
>
> In the meantime, again, really, I had a lovely time and I think you are a mensch and a very good man.

Flabbergasted by this strange turn, I immediately wrote back:

> Dear Vendetta, thanks for clarifying things. I figured something had gone haywire when I didn't hear back from you (evidence that there is such a thing as male intuition). At least I'm relieved that you weren't upset that I didn't insist you listen to *March of the Falsettos* or *Torch Song Trilogy*. Will you be staying on JDate, given your second thoughts about involvement?
>
> I can understand your concerns over distance and the flux in your life, which I see as the bigger issue, since your emotional energy is going to go into mortal divorce combat and concerns about your children as they play into the divorce. I can't get overly anxious about distance, since I was ready to throw myself into a relationship spanning 5,000 miles.
>
> By all means let's keep in touch. I like chatting with you, and now that we have phone numbers we can talk. Think of me as a friend, a resource, whatever you want. We really didn't even scratch the surface of conversation on Thursday, and it left me curious to hear more.

To my surprise, Vendetta sent a short note asking how things were going. I replied, in part,

> I'm sorry for the divorce situation. That may sound trite, but I feel for you and the kids. Nobody should have to face that kind of meanness, and I don't even know anything about it. I can tell the enormous psychic strain it puts on you, the sheer amount of energy it takes. It's bad enough that marriages end; does the aftermath have to go on and on?

We swapped a few more messages and then I never heard from her again, although I made a few attempts to connect. Her silence told me everything I needed to know. I turned my attention back to the Swan and others, the sources of so much functional value. The flow chart of yearning branched in one direction rather than the other.

And Vendetta? She stayed in my mind, as I wondered how her life evolved after our brief flicker of contact. I wish her well. She has her own stories to tell. I'm not one of them.

Portions of "His Perspective: The Functional Value of Heartache" were originally published in JMag, the online magazine for JDate.com.

Chapter 7

Speed Dating, or, The Shock of the Real

Dating sites often offer real-world events where people can actually meet and get acquainted. Some were "official" events; others were organized by site members on their own. In both cases, the experience was very different from grazing among the profiles. I was forced to interact in larger groups where I often felt out of place, out of my solitary element.

I wilted in loud, crowded, alcohol-driven venues where men were challenged to blast into a tight circle of women friends huddling together like a rugby scrum. Typically, the noise, the crowds, and the lack of information about the women inhibited me. I felt adrift and out of my element, just one more Jewish guy with a goatee trying to shout above the roar.

I hoped for a better experience in the more structured environment of speed dating, through a version organized by JDate's parent company, called HurryDate. I had never done anything like it. Compared to the micromanaging possible online—backstory provided by profiles, mood created by pictures, snappy rejoinders composed at the keyboard rather than on the spot—HurryDate promised to close the digital distance in real time, real space but with a chance to focus on one woman at a time. I wouldn't have to sidle up to a woman held in a tight little posse of her female friends, nor try to force myself into the line of tycoons (so I always imagined) angling for the proverbial Hot Jewish Chick. Participants had four minutes in the mixing bowl to figure that out, face to face.

I thought carefully about presentation. The women would see the 3-D me, not pictures. A slide show versus live theater. Deciding to go upscale, I wore a sports coat, a blue button-down shirt and a confidence-inspiring Jerry Garcia tie. The ensemble said, "I pay attention. You're worth a guy who dresses nicely for our first encounter."

I walked into the Falucka bar/restaurant on Bleecker Street in time for the half-hour of socializing. Scanning the group to check out the women—and the men—I signed in and settled into an open space at the bar to talk to a man who, like me, lived in the suburbs. He was there with a friend. They must not have liked the pickings, because they left before the event started.

The organizers gave the stragglers a few extra minutes; then they explained the mechanics: women stay seated, men move on every four minutes to the next table for a new date whenever a whistle was blown.

The first date started the HurryDate experience nicely. The woman was intelligent, educated, attractive. Information about her children suggested she was probably older than me, but I wasn't going to let that be a hindrance. I marked her "yes" on my score sheet, which offered only yes-and-no choices. HurryDate left no room for ambiguity.

As I moved through other dates, each conversation had its own rhythm. What do you do, where do you live, what do you enjoy doing in your spare time (I asked that, but nobody asked me). When the conversation lingered too long on a single topic, like our children, I asked another question. Several times I had to explain the origins of my highly un-Jewish name, Van.

I kept my eye on the approaching women as the whistle-signal led to another round of musical chairs. You see, I recognized two of the women. One I had dated a few times several years earlier, and another I had emailed on JDate and never received a reply. I had contacted her in recent weeks after she changed her picture—I told her I liked it—but I never heard back.

I rolled into a date with the no-contact woman first. I recognized her name, profession and look from her profile, where she had recently placed an appealing new picture. It had to be her. We did the usual getting-to-know-all-about-you chatter, then I said, "You know, I have written to you on JDate and you never responded." She explained she had had computer problems, and other people had also been concerned when they didn't hear back from her. Our conversation had more of an edge to it, based on a history, albeit one-sided one. I marked her a "yes."

My very next date was the woman I met on before. We went out a few times; then I got involved with someone else. She also remembered me, and even mentioned an old screen name. We knew enough to get caught up on work and kid issues, and that felt good. I marked her a "yes," also.

I kept moving around. The sound level rose, and after more than a dozen dates my energy flagged. I was relieved when I reached the last one, with a woman I had spoken to during the social hour.

At home, I logged on and cast my votes. I marked yes for four, no for the others (I would have marked only three, but two women had the same name and I couldn't tell from my notes which I was interested in, so I marked both). I couldn't fake enthusiasm for women where I felt no connection. I could tell when I would be interested, on emotional, social and, yes, physical grounds. After all the back and forth JDate often involves, an in-person meeting and a chance to see and hear really can make a difference. A day later, I had three "yes" matches—the three I wanted. The confidence-building Jerry Garcia tie had worked its magic.

The evening yielded one date, with the woman I had written to before. We had lunch in Greenwich Village and walked around outdoor art displays. Her photo had benefited from professional-level makeup, so she didn't look as I expected, and our personalities didn't fit at all. So that was that. I never tried HurryDate again.

However, the concept makes lots of sense for people who step away from their computer to meet people in the real world.

"Speed Dating, or, The Shock of the Real" was originally published in JMag, the online magazine for JDate.com.

Chapter 8

Brief Encounters, or, Ships Colliding in the Night

Compared to a painting style, online dating is more Jackson Pollock paint splotch than grand sweeping canvas. The big picture consisted of a mess of overlapping contacts, conversations, encounters, hopes, disappointments, laughter, driveway embraces, coincidences, betrayals and actual relationships. Some never got past an excruciating first meeting. Often nothing happened after a ho-hum first phone conversation. Some connections never got the chance to bloom or go as far as I hoped.

Some of my favorite stories don't fit neatly into a big-theme chapter. Something happened, a smile flashed and faded, I chased a purr that guttered into silence, I formed a friendship that has endured. Here, some dispatches from the love-war zone:

"Go ahead, ask me."

I wrote to one woman who sounded intelligent and committed to her beliefs, and I liked her pictures. I heard nothing. Then she was gone from JDate. About eight months later her profile returned and, ever the optimist, I IM'd her. We chatted and she invited me to call her, so I did. I didn't really think about the absence. People come and go all the time on dating sites as they fall in and out of love, get frustrated, or just lose interest for a time.

We talked a while and she finally said she had been off JDate. I said I had noticed.

"You can ask me why I was off JDate for six months."

I found this puzzling.

"Really, you can ask me."

Curious, I finally said, "Okay, why were you off JDate?"

"Because I was incarcerated!"

This led to a half-hour monologue for which I was an audience of one. In an increasingly strident tone, the woman related what exactly led to her spending six months in jail. She wasn't kidding, either; she said an article in a publication would tell the whole story and I found it as soon as it appeared. Making threats against public officials isn't a turn-on for me, so our contacts ended promptly then.

♥

My dating life intersected with the criminal justice system at least one other time. I wanted to meet Galadriel, whose nickname reflects her healing powers and her lovely flowing tresses that reminded me of the Elven princess Galadriel's in *The Lord of the Rings,* played by Cate Blanchett. Galadriel had three children and a busy schedule, so arranging a date was unusually difficult. But we were motivated and all systems were go for a Sunday afternoon at the Neuberger Museum on the campus of the State University of New York in Purchase. I was cruising along the Merritt Parkway getting close to SUNY when Galadriel called, sounding terribly upset.

"I can't meet you. I have to go pick up my kids at a police station in the Bronx."

"Good God, Galadriel, what happened?" I said, trying to keep from steering my car into a ditch.

"They were with their father at his apartment. He got

into a fight with his girlfriend and she called the police on him—domestic abuse. They all got taken to jail and the kids are just sitting there in the waiting room. I'm so sorry, I can't come meet you."

"That's totally okay. Your kids obviously come first." I turned around in the museum parking lot and headed back to Stamford, on the phone with Galadriel the whole time to keep her company and ease her anxiety as she sped down to the precinct house in the Bronx. I felt frustrated but understood the seriousness of the situation. Galadriel and I later met and I was a guest at a seder and Thanksgiving with her family. We're still friends.

♥

"You seem to be looking at me in an intense way."

Nicki's profile only had one picture, but I liked it. Her teasing attitude, something that always caught my attention, came through clearly. She talked about finding a good kisser, and I licked my lips at the possibility. I wrote,

> This should be a memorable Friday the Thirteenth, as Nicki and I meet this evening in Wilton. We spoke last night and she asked, "Do you kiss on the first date?" so she's more naughty by the minute. I have to see if she has stalkerish tendencies. I'm not used to this level of wild enthusiasm. Plus I need to see her from the neck down. But I've left the rest of the weekend open.

We arranged to meet on a summer weekend afternoon at the Starbucks in Wilton, Connecticut. I found the place and sat outside, waiting with that heart-thumping anticipation that comes from meeting an attractive prospect. Looks do count, after all.

Nicki finally sauntered up to my table. She looked even better than her picture. She wore tight jeans and a sleeveless top cut excruciatingly low, providing me an unnerving view of her cleavage. She gave me a warm hug.

We got our icy coffee drinks and chatted. At one point she said, "You seem to be looking at me very intensely." I shrugged it off with a non-committal answer. She was in a creative field, always a good sign, but something told me she gravitated more to the greasy biker types than an egghead like me. Still, we were giving it a chance. We strolled around downtown Wilton, a place with its share of hidden nooks and crannies for couples. Boldly (idiotically?) I held her hand and she seemed pleased or, at least, not completely repulsed. We found a bench and, completely out of character, I auditioned for the good kisser role.

We were in a jolly mood as I walked her back to her car. I could see getting together again and we agreed to do that. I decided to keep rolling the dice with Nicki.

"Am I looking at you less intensely?" I asked as we leaned against her car.

"Yes."

"I was looking that way so I wouldn't be staring at your cleavage," I admitted, which made her laugh. She was very provocative with the low-cut blouse and perky bosom—very upfront.

"Plus," I wrote, "she has a very strong Jewish identity, which gives us a lot of common ground."

Then: the old, old story. Calls and emails and IMs went nowhere. I finally got her on IM after plans for a birthday get-together with ice cream failed to happen:

> Van: Hey, Nicki what's happening? Did we crash and burn already?
> Nicki: No silly

> Van: Okay, I just like to check. I've missed our contacts.
> Nicki: Unbelievably busy at work. Getting home late and out early.
> Van: I'm saving the ice cream social for you.
> Nicki: Yummy
> Van: And of course birthday surprises.
> Nicki: LOL
> Van: You laugh, but I'm serious.
> Nicki: Really?
> Van: Sure. My big project on Sunday while you were working on getting the kids out of the house.
> Nicki: Ohhhhhhh .....
> Van: Don't worry, they won't melt.
> Nicki: Goodie!
> Van: I'll keep the batteries fresh. Of course I'll expect a surprised look on your face.
> Nicki: Well I'll remember that.

I never heard from her again. I didn't have a last name and I had deleted her phone number (a very unusual act for an information scavenger like me). I guess some greasy biker is enjoying that deliriously cantilevered bosom.

♥

Clash of the Elitists

Sometimes my journal tells a story so succinctly I might as well quote that. Here goes:

> I met Charmayne on Lafayette Street and we strolled around until we found a place to eat where she'd been before. She's an odd, opinionated duck—she bridled at my mention of the Right Stuff dating service, calling it "elitist," because she went to a

respected but non-Ivy state school in the Midwest.

"Well, even elitists need love," I said.

Then I told her about our plans for a bar mitzvah at Masada, which alarmed her as "Zionist." I should have spoken up, but I didn't want to inflame the conversation. She's plainly way to the left ....

♥

Car Wars I: Saab Stories

In New York City, cars never figured in my dating life. Subways and cabs moved me and my romantic interests around (although in rueful retrospect I could have sprung for cabs more often). In the suburbs, however, cars rule. Besides reliable transportation, they provide a rough guide to status and income potential.

After my divorce, I fell miserably short along both matrices of automotive excellence. I got the 1986 Saab 900, a red four-door that looked right at home in Fairfield Country, where half the cars at the time seemed to be distinctive Saabs. They have a great reputation for performance in snow and solidness in accidents, but my particular car had expensive repair bills and horrid reliability (I'm from South Texas. People in South Texas don't know Saabs at all; there's just not much need for a snow-savvy car on the windy flatlands of Hidalgo County).

The Saab had a nasty habit of stalling at stoplights, accelerated from zero to 30 mph in 60 seconds (offering great fun when I entered the Merritt Parkway and jostled with the Jaguars, Miatas and occasional Ferraris of the Masters of the Universe who roared past me) and sometimes just wouldn't start at all no matter how many times I finessed the key, opened and closed the doors and tried every trick I could imagine. Some of my worst moments as a new single dad came on Fridays when I was going to pick up my son—and my car wouldn't start. That led to some mighty uncomfortable conversations. Ultimately, I avoided the custodial headaches by renting cars on the weekend.

The car figured into the early years of my dating life, usually in a negative way. I dreaded the thought of driving too far from home on the off-chance that the Saab would conk out. Once a woman, Motek, and I were hot to meet each other, but she lived hundreds of miles away and I couldn't muster the nerve to actually drive up there to meet her—a missed opportunity I regretted. She later reminded me of this miscue. What could I say? For neither the first nor last time in my dating career, I failed to seize the day for a moronic reason.

The Saab fear was grounded in reality. I learned just how treacherous the car was when I took a date to fireworks on the Connecticut shore for the Fourth of July, 2004. After the event we headed to the Saab for the drive back to Stamford. The car started, then died. Nothing happened. It sat there like an inert piece of red, rusty iron. I was mortified. The police came to check on things. The woman, from Eastern Europe, took the episode in stride. I got AAA to come lug the car to a local repair place and my date and I took a cab back to Stamford.

Still, the car could perform well enough as a warm, enclosed space for conversations and other activities once a relationship had moved past the Starbucks stage. Dulce, mentioned earlier, and I used to bond in the front seat while the heating system strained to keep the frigid Connecticut beach weather at bay. In the summer of 2005, I finally bought a Hyundai Elantra. Finding a group to take the Saab as a donation proved more difficult than I expected, but ultimately Chabad of Great Neck came to Stamford to take the car off my hands, and the moment when the Saab rolled forever out of my sight was a time of great rejoicing—I was free at last from a car that held too many memories.

♥

Car Wars II: Carnal Knowledge

The year 2005 split my dating life into two parts. As the year started, I had a crappy car and lots of credit card debt. By the summer, I had reliable wheels in the form of a Hyundai Elantra and no credit card debt. The effect was immediate and exhilarating. I had the freedom to go places and actually enjoy myself rather than fret—and I am a fretter *par excellence*—about the impact of a date on my credit-card debt. Women can sense a man with money woes and I'm sure I gave off waves of money anxiety so long as I was juggling three credit cards with massive balance transfers. Suddenly that anxiety vanished, replaced by a sense of financial confidence and, even, generosity.

The Elantra let me hit the road in a new way. The car didn't stall, didn't wheeze, didn't give me headaches. It gave me four wheels and the open road to explore the region. Dating became much easier when I didn't have to sweat over another sad Saab stall story.

The car even gave me a conversation gambit and way to connect with other new car owners. Look at it this way: talking about a car that malfunctioned regularly would turn off anybody; talking about a smooth new ride speaks of good judgment, solid finances and a respectable lifestyle. Just two days after I happily wheeled away the Elantra, I wrote:

> I had a delightful chat with Singer, who looked at me, then I looked at her, we started a chat and switched to AIM. She's got a saucy side; we chatted about adolescence and she mentioned "strange

> erotic thoughts." That's a signal, all right. Then something about her new car, a VW, and sleeping in her car. I said, "Think about that when you slip into the rich leather seats of your new VW." I said my initials were VW. We agreed words are powerful and the movies of the '30s, '40s and '50s packed a sexual wallop by being less explicit.

Singer soon sang her swan song before we could act out scenes from Humphrey Bogart-Lauren Bacall movies—"You do know how to whistle, Jim? You just pucker your lips and blow" (*To Have and Have Not*)—but my new car served as a faithful sidekick in my dating adventures. What happened? Pull out your old LP by the singer Meat Loaf and listen to "Paradise by the Dashboard Light." That'll explain everything.

♥

The Tale of the Wonkish Cougar

Truth be told, Mrs. Robinson exuded sensuality in person but came across as a bit starchy online, a wonkish cougar, if you can imagine the combination. Chatting once, I asked impishly, "What turns you on?"

"Healthcare policy," she wrote back in all seriousness.

Still, she stoked my curiosity (I'm not calling her Mrs. Robinson for nothing). We talked about meeting when she visited New York for a wedding. She even made noises about me getting a tux and being her date at the upscale wedding, to which she promised to wear a very slinky gown. My imagination began to wander. The escort part, alas, fell through, but we still got together. As I wrote,

> I met Mrs. Robinson at the Essex House. She was already dressed to thrill in a sleeveless dress that was very low cut. She projected an electricity I

> found very attractive—lots of self-confidence in her appearance.
>
> "Your pictures on your profile don't do you justice," I said. I think she liked this. She's got a knock-out figure—that bust on display—and saucy look, bouncy blonde hair. I wanted to just munch on those shoulders. She talked too much about healthcare policy, but I steered her away from that. At some points I felt her foot brush against my leg.
>
> We strolled to Essex House. She told me about the famous dress, strapless, low-cut. I was dying. I have to see a picture of that.

I never saw the dress. Still, she fired my imagination. I envisioned us in our very own swashbuckling romance novel. I would be her hairy-eared Fabio and she would be my flushed, ruby-lipped pirate queen. Together we would point the prow of her curving bodice toward the great passion of her life—discussions of healthcare policy reforms. A year later, I visited the city where Mrs. Robinson lived and we planned to meet. I had visions of a romantic walk under the spring foliage, but as I hit the city limits she called to cancel because of a family matter. I could taste the metallic disappointment in my mouth. I checked in several times during the crisis, but I finally gave up.

♥

The Shabbat Seductress

Sometimes, the magic happened. Timing, inclination, location, daring, attraction and the alignment of the stars combined to move me speedily up the online dating curve. At those moments, the good angels locked their wings together, lay down their ever-turning flaming swords and opened the gates to the Garden of Eden for biblical bonding. One woman who regularly visited New York contacted me and we met for a Friday night service at the Carlebach Shul on the Upper West Side, known for its rollicking Orthodox services. After that, we returned to the apartment where this Shabbat Seductress was staying. I wrote,

> Services lasted a loud, long time, so we didn't return to the apartment until ten. I imagined we'd have coffee, a nosh and I'd be on my merry way, but that was not exactly the agenda, as the Passoveresque Shabbat food kept flowing out of the kitchen—matzoh ball soup, salad—and the night lingered on. Well, that's what Shabbat is all about, as she stressed relaxation ... We listened to a lot of music. I don't call Chet Baker "smooch jazz" for nothing. Anyway ... I finally bolted and barely made the 1:07 a.m. train back here.
>
> A few days later we toured the Fairway supermarket, which she adores, and I had never seen. "Find something you want for breakfast," she said casually.
>
> "Oh, aren't you the rascal," I said.
>
> "I thought you knew," she replied.
>
> Really, I'm such an innocent. I had no idea that would happen. We strolled up to the apartment and once inside got down to kissyface pretty efficiently, powered by more CDs.
>
> Shabbat 'n' Chet Baker smooch jazz—what a winning combination.

The Shabbat Seductress and I became warm friends and shared holiday adventures in deepest Brooklyn, and have even collaborated on some editorial projects.

♥

Fedelma the Oenophile

Fedelma and I exchanged fun banter about our backgrounds. I pointed her to some online reading and she referred to the "Hebrew-Hibernian article—a sweet little tribute to *two tribes* with a theatrical bent." Our emails indeed had a literary bent. So we finally got together for a first date at the Guggenheim Museum in New York. After the stroll down the spiral display area of the museum, we went to a French restaurant for dinner on the Upper East Side. Now French food is a type I almost never eat, preferring Indian, Chinese, Cuban, Mexican, Thai and BBQ. I can't remember what I ordered, but I do remember the meal came with a choice of hot cider or wine to drink. Fedelma chose the wine, I chose the cider, not having any genetic predisposition to alcohol (if I could have ordered a sweet, sticky alcoholic drink with an umbrella in it, that would have been a different story).

A day or two later we had a post-date conversation and Fedelma voiced deep concern. I thought the first contact went well enough. Fedelma couldn't understand why I wanted the cider rather than the wine. Who eats French food without fine wine? I could tell we were running on tracks that would never intersect, all because I had such a Baptist preference for nonalcoholic drinks. We never met again.

♥

Screwing Up With Motek

I met Motek early on and we connected in a strong way. She called me special and said my ability to "read" her was scary. I hinted how she could "read" me with motivations like letting me feel wanted and accepted. But I dithered and dawdled on meeting her because of my creaky 1986 Saab, which kept me locked up hundreds of miles from her. Of course, the onrushing rapids of romance soon carried her far away:

I haven't heard from Motek in a couple of days so I know she's out there dating. I called, in a blaze of creativity, her home. Her daughter said to try the cell. I did, against my better judgment, and got through to her. She couldn't tell who it was—she was in a restaurant. Before long she did IM, telling me she was with an Israeli pilot. I felt embarrassed at my failure of judgment, which was flagrant—my gut had told me not to call. She didn't seem fazed. She felt odd, telling me, calling him the "competition." ...

[A few days later]

We had glorious chats of rising intensity but my exquisitely timed phone call and the talk that followed gave me some clues to the current context: Israeli pilot, around for two weeks, intriguing and sexy and there, well, why not have a great fast fling? Let nature take its course. Still, even I had visions of sugar plum fairies, and Motek and I are so much on the same wavelength.

[A few days after that]

Motek seems to have completely withdrawn from the field of combat—sad, because we had a strong connection even if she [catty comment redacted]. Other things beckon. And I was the one that said I wouldn't disappear. The chain of connection is so fragile, but new chains are always being forged. I was on the phone last night for an hour with the Girl from Ipanema in Brazil. She speaks amazingly good English, very colloquial, as if she lived here. So, that was fun.

♥

Listen Only

The Lark and I always had a great friendship. As soon as we met we began swapping chatty notes, often on our romantic frustrations with others. I advised her on the mating habits of Southern men, while she provided empathetic play-by-play analysis of my thwarted pursuits. She lived in Boston and worked as a health-care professional, but we never could navigate the New England space between us.

Finally, however, the stars aligned. We arranged to meet in Boston, where I would be on a business trip for several days. I took Amtrak up the day before to settle into my hotel and then stroll around the Harvard campus. I sat on the steps of a building, looking at the students and parents, and thought life was pretty good. An interested project beckoned; the Lark and I would finally meet, and the mid-summer weather made me think of Robert Frost poetry.

The next day I bopped to my company's Boston office and waited for other team members to arrive from New York for a big marketing project. I noted an email about a conference call at 11:30, something about changes in the marketing function. I knew executives had been examining the department, and I figured there would be people coming and going, shifting boxes on the org chart, nothing dramatic.

My colleagues from New York breezed in at 11:25, with just enough time to grab a cup of coffee and settle in for the call, which, oddly enough, was listen-only. Nobody could talk, only listen.

We dialed in and the speaker got right to the point. Our marketing function hadn't been working the way the leaders wanted and the company was going in a new direction for the work we did. Our services were no longer needed. We would be hearing from HR.

End of call.

Lark's Lament: Instead of dinner with the Lark, I packed up my former office, including the Russian and Yiddish posters seen on the wall.

We sat there, stupefied. All of us had been laid off. Almost our entire department, nationwide, was wiped out in a listen-only conference call that lasted only four minutes.

As you can imagine, chaos ensued. We had to tell the client-facing team in the Boston office we had just been laid off and couldn't work on the project. Our cellphones hummed as we frantically called family members and rearranged our travel plans. I called the Lark and told her that our plans were star-crossed and that dinner would have to wait. She was as disappointed as I was, but understood completely. I called other obscure objects of thwarted affection and left voice mails about the Beantown slaughter so they would feel sorry for me and want to talk to me (and they did, as I turned lemons into lemonade).

I returned to New York and found myself in demand for job interviews, given my skill set. I had a first call from one firm on September 11, of all days, and began working there in October on my birthday, of all days. The spell of unemployment passed quickly. Another year would pass before the Lark and I would finally meet in Mystic, Connecticut, but we connected and have met several times since then. We are both good listeners.

Meanwhile, the Listen-Only Massacre became a dark legend in New York professional-services circles. Marketers and headhunters talk about it with horrified fascination to this day.

❤

The Divine Miz R Politely Requests the Presence of Your Company

Miz Rutherford and I connected in that regional U.S. way, given her gracious Southern upbringing in the land of moss-drenched oaks, mint juleps, firefly-watching from the front porch, black-eyed peas on New Year's Day (Jan. 1, not Rosh Hashanah), expressions of "Land sakes alive, honey chil'!" and Lynyrd Skynyrd albums.

Both of us fell off the turnip truck and landed in Gotham City decades ago. Miz Rutherford (AKA The Divine Miz R) has lived in the Northeast as long as I have and fits right in to

Yankeeland. But once we met, the Southernisms became a running joke throughout our friendship.

My first date with Miz Rutherford proved memorable. We got together on a Friday after work for a light dinner at an outdoor café, nothing unusual about that, but she had also asked me if I wanted to go to "something else." She was a little cagey about what exactly "something else" was. Something thought provoking, perhaps emotionally challenging. As a veteran of a long-running men's group and even some twelve-step meetings, I was open to the idea. I agreed to go and didn't ask too many questions. In fact, I didn't want Miz Rutherford to tell me much at all. I had plenty of time for a Friday event, and I didn't mind a mysterious, madcap Manhattan adventure. My main thought: would we be taking our clothes off? Would the event involve drippings of hot wax or vampire worship?

Miz Rutherford and I wandered to an Upper East Side apartment already crowded with people who looked, well, like people anywhere in New York. Some old, some young, couples, singles. I paid a door fee and Miz Rutherford and I squeezed into some open space.

I'll end the mystery: Miz Rutherford and I attended an "encounter group" called the Mark Group. Started in California in the 1960s, the movement brings people together for guided discussions of issues and exercises that encourage self-revelation. The others talked about lifestyle choices that are way down the road from my boring suburban patterns (on the continuum of sensual lifestyles, I'm the poster boy for the conventional concept of "vanilla"; they're more "Dark Odyssey"). I'll respect the rules of confidentiality and not reveal specifics, but I did indeed find the evening emotionally challenging, as to what to reveal and what to hide, and whether to deceive. Miz Rutherford told a little fib about how we knew each other, but that was acceptable under the ground rules.

Everybody kept their clothes on, nobody dripped wax on me. I never attended another Mark Group meeting, but I still think back on the surprising adventure that definitely pushed me outside my comfort zone of typical first dates. I give The Divine Miz R a lot of credit for instinctively knowing I would be okay with a Mark Group meeting. It must be a Southern thang.

Chapter 9

Running the Numbers of Romance

E pluribus unum—out of many, one. That motto found on U.S. currency also applies to online dating. Out of many opportunities, find the one.

The connection to currency is deliberate and relates to a side of dating I tracked in my obsessive-compulsive way: the investment. What did I spend in my search for love and its more earthy equivalents? What did I get in return, and how did I calculate my ROEI—Return on Emotional Investment? The basic answers are easy to determine; during the entire time I've been single I've used one bank account and one credit card. Usually when I incurred a dating expense, I noted the event and the woman involved in my Quicken software program. Put the event (usually dinner) and a name together and I can get a sharp mental image of an encounter.

- Bangkok Imperial in New Haven, K, $41.90. We hit it off. She had studied Russian and had red hair. But she was looking for a man without young children, so that never happened.
- Oest Restaurant in New York, L, $68.70. My first date with a fellow Princetonian. Nice Sunday brunch. We had one more date volunteering at a Jewish event, then nothing.

- Free Times Café in Toronto, klezmer brunch, $33.36. My jaunt north of the border. Nice but no magic.
- Akdeniz Restaurant in New York, Turkish food for lunch with F from Latin America. She was a corporate executive who kept checking her BlackBerry. We were doomed.
- Roger Smith Hotel, wine with E, first and only meeting with a mental-health professional from Mexico visiting New York. I got photos of us together—and a good thing I did because our contacts completely fizzled after that.
- Cabana Midtown, Cuban food with S from Italy. She was an exotic type involved in fashion. She started crying and said I looked like her late father.
- Hummus Place, somewhere on the Upper West Side. My notation says "J Dogs?" because she liked to talk about her dogs. $28.36.

The names and dates roll on and on: Dvora at Wave Hill, Joan at Tintol, Galadriel at Stone Cold Creamery in Stamford. A date, a name, a place—each one combines to evoke a snippet of theater, a memory of friendship made and roads looked down but not taken.

Then there were the dating sites. I started with Jcupid, paying $99.95 on February 27, 2003. I was on and off JDate for nineteen months between 2003 and 2008, long enough to see the monthly charge rise from $28.50 to $39.99. Total expenditure: $640. Total number of emails sent: around 3,000; received: 2,000.

I also used Match, which had a thriftier cost structure and a fair amount of overlap with JDate's membership. The per-month cost was lower, and the site allowed for longer essays and a lot more photos, both of which appealed to my strong points of writing and hey-look-at-me photography. Whatever I am, I was never shy about self-revelation online, and Match let me play that up. Total investment: $440. Emails sent: can't tell (Match emails are erased after a certain amount of time); emails received: around 600.

Through it all, I can vouch for the song saying that, "romance without finance" won't work out. For the first two-plus years of my single life, I struggled with post-divorce credit card debt into the five figures. I chipped away at the total (tracking the agonizingly slow progress on Quicken, of course), but I still didn't have the cash for a swinging social life. All it took was one big repair on my creaky, clanky 1986 Saab sedan to throw my financial progress into reverse. I found the resources to fly down to Brazil, but otherwise I felt constrained.

My financial profile changed dramatically when I paid off the credit cards. I could finally take a deep breath, crank up my 401(k) contributions and think about how I could manage a real pursuit opportunity. The records show a sharp increase in spending as I often followed one date with another a day or two later. On one February 1, I ate at McArthur's American Grill with Joan. On Feb. 6 I ate at the Evergreen Shanghai Restaurant in New York with one woman; the next day I ate at the same place with a Princeton friend I'd pined for two decades earlier (until we got together for Chinese food in Greenwich Village and she started chatting about her boyfriend).

> Van to L: It's been a while since I got your email on JDate. I'm sorry things didn't work out between us—like you, I don't know what else to say. I'll always remember our Manhattan pub crawl and Brazilian music.

One enjoyable component of the ROEI is gift giving. Usually I have a knack for good surprises: flowers, a silk scarf, theater tickets. I improved over the years after some horrendous clunkers in the past. Sometimes my instinct failed me and I generate bad karma; in one case, the gift remained ungiven for years due to circumstances beyond my control. To wit:

> I met with coworkers Bo, Peter, Lianne and Joanne at a bar at 7 Rivington Street. They wanted to hear my tales of woe and that was helpful. I left enough time to go by Babeland at 94 Rivington at Ludlow to get the Weil 7-in-1 vibrator kit. I wanted to get it for Mala but the way things are going it may tickle the fancy of a lady yet unknown.

I bought the mighty Weil for $39.02 (I saved the receipt), using a corporate gift card. My doleful prediction came true; I never gave it to Mala, and the longer it sat in my closet, the less inclined I was to present it to anybody. It just didn't seem right. So it just stays on the shelf next to the floss and light bulbs. If anybody wants a pristine, unopened (really!) vibrator, gently wrapped in unrequited dreams, just let me know and we'll arrange a handoff.

How do I define ROEI, return on emotional investment? The crudest, most obvious measurement would be cost per sexual encounter. However, that doesn't capture the range of value a relationship can deliver. I like to think a relationship, even if it stays at the level of friendship, provides something worthwhile. If sex is the only payoff, then that's a recipe for a wretched ROEI. So we could start with a denominator being the total dollar amount spent. The nominator would combine the positive and negative aspects of the relationship. That would be the cube of the number of Passover seders, Fourth of July BBQs, Thanksgivings and birthdays observed together, plus (number of cuddly encounters times the value of pi) minus number of angry discussions of the status of the relationship times number of breakups.

Inasmuch as I flunked calculus at Princeton, I'm the wrong guy to devise a mathematically precise quantitative analysis for ROEI. The concept works best as a descriptor of a relationship. In some I made a huge emotional investment and got almost nothing back; let's call that my Madoff madness, throwing emotional capital into an opportunity long after I should have taken my losses and pulled the plug. Then others rewarded my good judgment and pay dividends regularly.

The intellectual delights of ROEI finally faded away. I just stopped caring—for the best reason. For the last four years I've been in a relationship that works well and I don't even try to figure the ROEI. That's one of the nicest parts of a stable relationship—the numbers stop mattering when the living works out.

The Modern Portfolio Theory of Dating

In addition to ROEI, my years in the dating jungle led me to develop another useful framework. Somewhere in my ill-spent years as an economics major at Princeton, I learned the concept of investment diversification, or modern portfolio theory. That means, in essence, don't put all your eggs into one basket. By spreading your investments among different options, you lower the relative volatility of your portfolio (the "beta") and have a more stable rate of return. You can either aim to focus on maximizing return or minimizing risk. So go ahead and have a fling on a dot-com start-up or sub-prime mortgage fund, but don't skimp on the index funds and Dow Jones industrials.

In my madder days of dating, I thought of my activities

as an exercise in portfolio theory.

I'll admit that the goal of a dating strategy runs exactly opposite of real portfolio theory. Dating strategy for most people aims to find the *beshert,* the one man or woman to whom you commit and cherish. Financial portfolio theory means you forsake the one for the many, holding and adjusting a basket of diversified investments that, so the theory goes, will not all go up and down at the same time. Some rise, some fall, but the result is you never get totally hosed. In real life, I do that with investments in stock and bond index funds.

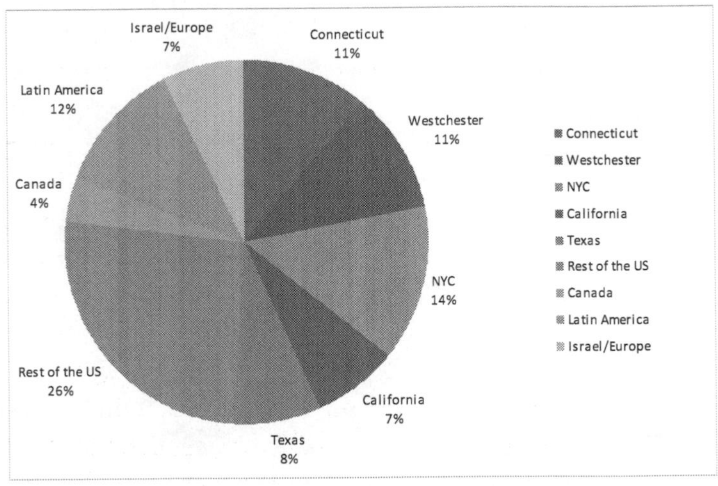

The dating portfolio theory at work, showing the percentage distribution of successful contacts by region.

In the online dating world, I didn't know what would work. I didn't want to remarry right away; it took years to even hold hands with a woman. While some people bring a laser-like focus to online dating—locals only, marriage-minded, must want children, can't have young children, and must keep kosher are among the valid limitations—I didn't set hard limits. I had a pretty clear idea of the kind of woman who appealed to me and I would look for them all over. No location was too far or too close. I was in touch with one woman who actually lived in my apartment building in Connecticut—we swapped emails and waved to each other in the basement laundry room but never mustered enough enthusiasm for even a cup of coffee. Yet, I flew 5,000 miles to Brazil to spend a week with a woman. In between these extremes, I had contacts with women all over the world—Israel, Canada, Latin America, California, Florida, Texas. So I diversified my dating portfolio to enhance returns rather than limit risks. I took some risks, and, looking back, heck, I should have taken a few more. If one prospect bitterly disappointed me, I had others in the pipeline. That might be a formula for emotional chaos, but diversification kept any one flame-out from leaving me feeling totally crushed (in theory, anyway).

I was so diverse I didn't know if I was coming or going. Had I possessed unlimited funds and leisure, I could have devoted all my time to world dating travel, hitting synagogues globally in the process. Moldovans in Silicon Valley, Romanians in Texas, Texans in New York, New Yorkers in Israel, Israelis in Westchester County, Mexicans in Canada, and all the Girls from Ipanema—our circles intersected and sometimes we actually met. When not wracked with despair, I had fun.

Looking back, I made some good friends through the portfolio approach. Relationships developed, although many were hampered by distance.

And that gets to the crux, perhaps, of why I expended so much energy scouring the world. Distance—keep them at arm's length, always have a reason for not meeting. While some couples make long-distance romance work, they ultimately need to close the distance for the relationship to thrive. Otherwise, a frustration factor kicks in. If children and custody schedules enter the mix of issues, the balancing act becomes even more difficult. My rule of thumb might be that two hours' travel sets the outer limit for a workable relationship. Beyond that, the process gets far iffier.

When I finally found a relationship that became stable, close and enjoyable, the woman lived forty-five minutes away. She was born in the United States. English is her first language. We both graduated from Ivy League schools in the same year. After all my wanderings, I found success close to home, rather than close to the Equator. The beta in my dating portfolio vanished as an issue—now, if only my real-world 401(k) performed so well!

Hearts driven far afield: Stumbling upon a celebration in Mexico.

Chapter 10

The Love File and How It Grew, or, Adventures in Emotional Archeology

Online dating fit well with my personality. It meshed with my sharp sense of self-knowledge and self-promotion. I knew how to describe myself in terms that appealed to certain kinds of women. That's what every guy hopes to do, but I knew how to hit the Jewish, Southern and literary angles that were catnip to certain women. That knack for sincere self-expression was the secret weapon that helped me at least get my foot in the dating door. Whether the door subsequently was slammed in my face is another issue.

Online dating also was a great fit with another quirky side of me: my relentless desire to document my life. This collecting and categorizing no doubt stemmed from a childhood desire to make sense of the world, to record my impressions and ease the growing isolation I felt growing up. I never knew my grandparents, for example, and I was determined to create my own history for later generations to read. From the age of twelve, I reported on my own life in a journal.

Besides the journal, I kept files of my literary works. In 1973 I started a literary folder called "Projects, et. al." to hold poems I had written like "Junkie's Lament," "A Watergate Trilogy," and "Faded Ponies on a Merry-Go-Round." Short stories included "Our Trip to the Mortuary," about an imagined grade-school field trip, and its delightful sequel, "Our Trip to Reynosa," about a sleazy town on the south side of the Texas-Mexico border.

The folder held melancholy teenage poems like "Just Friends" and this note from November 1972. Probably stuck in my locker at Mission High School, it sounds remarkably like emails I would linger over thirty-five years later:

> Van, it is late! I am just thinking about your call. I want you to understand that I have nothing against you and I would have gone to Homecoming. But understand a girl needs time to get ready and make plans. Believe me, Van, I'd love going with you but—but … I don't know how to put it. Van please excuse my writing as well as this letter. I mean I don't have a way with words! Okay? If you would have asked me a week before I would have gone with you. I like you as a friend Van. I want you to understand that! I think you're swell. I really dig you. And I hope you and I can become best friends. Also understand that I have a crush on [name redacted] and I can't help that. But I really do like you. Van I hope that you and I can become pals and whenever you have a problem I am here to help! I hope this goes the same for me! Thanks for asking me!

My life and interests evolved. After I left Texas for Princeton and then New York, I had regular (as in, required!) mail correspondence with my mother. I saved every letter she ever sent me, and made carbon copies of letters I wrote to her on IBM Selectric typewriters in the pre-desktop publishing era.

When I arrived in New York, I followed "Projects et al."

with a manila folder dubbed "The Love File"—a record of my search for romance. The idea struck me in June of 1980, during the weeks after I graduated from Princeton and moved to Brooklyn. I read an article in *New York* magazine, "A First Avenue Romance," about the adventures of twenty-somethings Barry and Debbie in the New York singles scene. The article whispered about the potential of my new urban life after affection-deprived college years. I thought, "I've got to hang on to this for future reference."

For eight years, the Love File swelled with articles, letters and pictures related to my quest for connection. Meandering through its pages, I feel like an emotional archeologist. Every scrap of material hints at my hopes and anxieties. The files include articles that rocked nervous singles of the mid-'80s, such as the notorious *Newsweek* "Marriage Crunch" cover article from June 1986 warning that college-educated women "still single at the age of thirty-five have only a five percent chance of ever getting married."

Maybe the Love File reflects my highly literal mindset: if part of my life exists in a tangible, printed form, then it really did happen. The quip of late *New York Times* columnist James Reston describes me perfectly: "How do I know what I think until I read what I write?" I never did trust my memory, hence my reliance on a camera, a journal, a letter to capture the light of an incandescent moment of high feeling. I don't want to die having forgotten my memories; rather, I want them to surround and wash over me and testify that, yes, I did all that.

The Love File helped me make sense of the experimentation and turmoil in which I tumbled. The contents remind me that I had relationships and that, however lonely I felt, I had plenty of company in my frustrations on the New York social scene.

Every clipping tells a story about a time and a

relationship. *New York* magazine's "Single Forever?" issue, from the summer of 1984, turbocharged the angst of a woman I was dating who had just turned thirty. I observed how her life played out, as she soon married and moved to Long Island. Endless iterations of the man shortage coldly amused me, as I faced the more relevant woman shortage. One favorite was "Older Women are Pooling Their Male Resources," from the *New York Times* of Feb. 5, 1986. Even the *Village Voice* chimed in with a round-up of books in February 1986, with the story, "The Mensch Shortage: Or, What Do Women Want?"

In those pre-digital days, most Love File items came from newspapers and magazines. I didn't save copies of the letters I wrote to *New York* and *Village Voice* ads. Personal items include a stack of birthday and Valentine's Day cards and scrumptious morning-after notes tied in twine in the Love File Annex. I've got the wedding announcement, sent by my mother, of a woman I dated in the Bicentennial summer of 1976.

An envelope holds photos of women I dated, with names like Shulamith, Adina, Joanne and Amy. I threw in an item I submitted to the *New York Times*' "Metropolitan Diary" that was never published, as well as a letter I wrote to relationship columnist Susan Dietz. I pushed the file's contents back to July 22, 1976 with a photo I took of a high school friend competing in a beauty contest.

The Love File swelled between 1986 and 1988 as I approached and then passed my thirtieth birthday. I saved a profile of actress-director Melanie Mayron, who battled Amy Irving in my mind for the title of Sexiest Jewish Woman Alive. AIDS and condoms articles appeared, as men and women negotiated terrifying new realities. Parenting articles such as "Older Parents' Child: Growing Up Special," from the *New York Times* of January 26, 1987, became relevant as I gamely looked ahead to marriage and fatherhood while approaching my thirtieth birthday.

Then I found the woman I would marry, and the collecting mostly stopped. Why clip those angst-wracked articles, when I had my *beshert* (Yiddish for "intended one") with me daily, nightly? Some final articles dribbled into the Love File as the '80s became the '90s. Whatever was published in the next decade passed me by. Marriage freed me from the need to worry about how the trends of single life warped my life. I was looking no more.

Alas, the Love File commented on my married life as it unfolded, refolded and fell apart. I clipped Dear Abby's column on "Ten Commandments for a Successful Marriage" from the *New York Post* on Valentine's Day, 1992. I prayed it would work like a rabbit's foot, a four-leaf clover, or a rattlesnake's tail, with lessons to help us in a marriage beset by crises. For years I carried it in my wallet, until it became so worn I transferred it to a binder that holds insurance policies, my birth certificate, my passport and other important papers.

I edged into dating several months after I moved out of the house in late 2002. I found that the dating game had changed drastically while I was married. Forget personal ads in the back of magazines; online dating sites had taken over. This paperless virtual world challenged my notion of the Love File. My drive to document remained strong. However, I would no longer clip ads from the Personals section of *New York* magazine, paste them in a journal and note the day when a woman responded, a process that took weeks. By the time a woman called, I could barely remember what her four-line profile said.

Online profiles gave far more information and even pictures, but they only existed on my computer screen. Our emails and chats flashed like lightning; they were there and then gone unless a site saved them. While Match deleted emails after a month, I did get an emailed copy of each one, which of course I always kept. JDate stored all messages indefinitely, so I could sort emails from special women into their very own folders so I could either delight or brood over them any time I wanted, so long as I paid for full access to the site. This was heaven on earth for a scrupulous sorter and sifter of romantic longings.

But I had a problem with JDate: without a paid membership, I had no access to emails. In response, the Love File moved in a radical direction. I began to print out some profiles and emails. Not all of them—I'm not *that* obsessive-compulsive. I only saved those with visual, psychic or sentimental appeal. The sheer amount of paper soon equaled years of Love File accumulation. Stuffing more materials into that bulging folder made no sense, nor did starting a new manila folder. The solution: I punched holes in the print-outs and slipped the pages into three-ring binders.

The initial, physically limited Love File has evolved into the open-ended Love File 2.0.

The binders recreate in print the digital reality of my dating days, with profiles and letters. They can trace the rise and crash of relationships from the first tentative "Hi, I connected with your profile on many levels, so that tells me to write to you ... just write back and we'll see what happens" through sharing and meeting to my hopeful "I had a great time, let's do it again soon" notes. The collections can be painful to read in retrospect, knowing how some encounters ended—with messages such as, "I know how you hate long silences."

> I tried calling your cell phone but the mailbox is full. I wanted to see if you were able to see the photos from Sunday. I liked them—our feet

> propped up was clever. Did you show Malka the proof that we did indeed get together?

My Love File folders expanded and provided raw material for this book. The stack grew to rival the heft of the Federal Tax Code. With a printer and enough ink, I could document my dating life to my heart's delight. An insightful therapist might ask whether the energetic collecting was one more way to put distance between myself and painful emotions. I would reply—yes, and the collection would be useful when I got around to writing a book about online dating.

Once I started dating a woman steadily, I let my site subscriptions lapse and I stopped printing profiles and emails. I did tear out an article from the Valentine's Day 2011 issue of the *Village Voice* about the travails of women in New York as a reminder of the hardiness of the literary genre of women's romantic woes in the big dirty city. Otherwise, the Love File captures a moment in my life, rather than a reflection of my current reality. I hardly ever look at the Love File, much less add to it. As with the time during my marriage, research on the singles life is pointless.

Why read when I can live?

Chapter 11

Visitors, Her Place and Mine

Living in a Connecticut suburb made me GU—geographically undesirable—for many women in New York City. I saw the logic; the train schedule set the rhythm of relationships when I dated there, for I had to calculate the time needed to reach Grand Central and settle in, gritty-eyed, for the late train to Stamford. The only way around that was to not let the date end. And that was a whole 'nother issue.

However, my location took on another meaning when women I knew visited New York. I might be in the suburbs but, compared to the Jewish male situation in some women's cities, I was right where they wanted me to be. For vacations and Jewish holidays, women cycled through New York and when they did, I could be there.

Over the years, I met a dozen women when they visited New York. One even stayed with me, although our relationship remained as pure as the driven snow, despite some ludicrous expectations on my part, quickly squashed.

♥

"Wanna be my bar mitzvah date?"

One woman I'll nickname Peaches and I actually had the rarest of confluences—we met in her city and later in New York. We first met on her home territory in one of my most amusing dating stories. I had flown to Atlanta one December for business. My colleagues and I planned to stay for several days, fly back to New York to recover for the weekend, then return to Atlanta to finish the project.

I was already in touch with Peaches and had let her know I would be in Atlanta, where she lived. Given the intense nature of the project—a dawn-to-past-dusk way to make a living, especially on the road—we couldn't find time to meet. Still, I kept her informed.

Then on Friday a major snowstorm hit New York. My colleagues and I monitored the weather and changed our flight plans to Saturday morning. Sitting in the restaurant at our hotel having a high-calorie waffle breakfast, I saw my options, if not my waistline, shrink. The corporate travel office representative said we could get a flight into New York, but she couldn't guarantee, because of the weather disruptions, that we'd be able to return to Atlanta. That settled it: we would stay in Atlanta for the weekend.

Back in my room I immediately called Peaches. The weekend loomed. I told her about my situation and the vast vistas of time that suddenly spread before me.

"Wanna be my date at a bar mitzvah?" she asked. She was attending one in an Atlanta suburb that very evening.

"Sure!" I said. I would meet her at a suburban temple for the party.

Attending an upscale Southern bar mitzvah hadn't been on my mind when I packed for Atlanta. I found myself woefully underdressed for the event. Undaunted, I hopped on the local subway system and headed for a mall to upscale my ensemble for the night.

This being Atlanta in the fall, I just happened to stumble upon the highlight of the football season, the big game between Georgia and LSU. Thousands of fans in their respective colors crowded the streets, good-naturedly ribbing one another. The scene on the MARTA was like a middle-aged version of *West Side Story*, with Bulldogs and Cajuns as understudies for the Sharks and the Jets.

At the mall I nosed around and settled on a black sweater. It would, at least, cover me up and provide some warmth. Back at the hotel, I found the football game had ended, in LSU's favor. I got in a cab, gave the address to the temple and settled in for the quiet ride.

But *quiet* it was not. I got a talkative driver, who learned I was a former journalist and writer. He connected that to a book he had read, *The Case for Christ*, by another novelist who set out to debunk the Gospels and instead found himself believing them. I politely listened to this for about twenty minutes, including a few rounds of driving aimlessly trying to find the temple. We finally arrived, to my relief. I wanted to snap, "Man, I'm past all that. I've got a brand new bag now," but I wisely held my tongue.

I had never met Peaches and had seen only one picture of her. I went into the temple, where crowds already milled about. Where was she? I went outside into the cool—nay, freezing—Georgia night to call my son for his traditional goodnight conversation.

I wasn't sure what to say through my chattering teeth. My social and dating lives ordinarily stay well apart. Tell him I'm at a bar mitzvah with a stranger who had yet to arrive? I kept the conversation light and not specific. That wasn't so hard.

I waited inside to keep frostbite from nipping my fingers, toes and nose. Peaches, quite recognizable, arrived and we greeted each other. She was that dating rarity—a woman significantly shorter, enough to make me look tall. We talked and she broke off to mingle with people she knew through her work in the community. The black sweater made me feel anonymous enough. We ate, talked, ate some more. She introduced me to people and I had somebody take photos of us. She said a friend later commented, "Aren't you a cute couple!"

The delicate matter of what we would do post-party hovered over us. Nobody at the suburban synagogue was heading downtown. As the last people who still lingered at the temple other than the cleaning crew, we finally called a cab for me. I waited, and waited, and waited, calling the company several times on my cell phone to see when they might grace me with their presence.

Finally, after a lonely forty-five minute wait—Peaches had gone home—a cab rolled up and we headed to Atlanta. No Christian driver this time. The new one played Middle Eastern music; I wondered what he thought about a temple pickup, but he didn't say anything.

The total fares for my night of adventure came to $90. I put every dime of it on my expense report and got reimbursed, no questions asked. A few months later, these expenses would not have been allowed. My night at the temple became a legend among my coworkers.

Years later, Peaches came to New York for several weeks. Now I got to play host. We hadn't really kept in touch, except for yearly emails, but I still remembered the chilly bar mitzvah so we met twice. The first time was at South Street Seaport for a Latin music evening. Before long we shrugged off the music and found an outdoor restaurant, as windy on that summer day as Atlanta had been cold. We talked and took the subway together until she peeled off at a stop near the apartment where she was staying. We met again for lunch near my office, at my favorite lunch-date hangout, a diner across the street from St. Patrick's Cathedral. Nothing happened, although I wonder if we could have glided into a back-clawing madcap Manhattan escapade. "Seize the day" has never been easy for me to adopt as a romantic philosophy. More like "Wait a couple of days."

The Woman from Farfarawayland

While nothing romantic happened with Peaches, I still have warm memories of our times together, both in New York and Atlanta. I can't say the same about other visitors to New York. One showed my tendency toward wishful thinking in encounters and inability to cut my losses in a bad situation.

This was my very first visitor, a woman from a magical place I'll call Farfarawayland. Let's call her Hecuba. Online, she had an alluring air. I looked at her exotic pictures and let my imagination run away with me, the possibilities of a relationship with a beauty raised near the dark, mutinous waves lapping at Farfarawayland. She had been to the U.S. before and had relatives here. Then, as often happens in relationships with terminals thousands of miles apart, the allure or newness ended and we stopped communicating. I felt she led me on, then let me down, something about another boyfriend. So be it.

Then one day in May I had a phone call from Hecuba. She was in Newark, N.J., planning to see relatives. Wishful thinking kicked in and I practically begged her to come into the city for dinner. She agreed, and we met at a sushi restaurant on Third Avenue. From the beginning, something didn't feel right. Was it the foreignness, my own stumbling early efforts at dating, a mismatch of personalities? Perhaps all these factors. She talked about a boyfriend. I wanted her to focus on me, not somebody else. She was okay staying at a hotel near the airport, but I was eager to have her stay with me in Connecticut, so she could be near her relatives. She finally agreed and I drove to Newark one sunny Sunday in my ratty and rattling 1986 Saab.

I found Hecuba in the lobby of the hotel with an enormous, weighty suitcase. I knew she had something big, but this approached steamer trunk size. Somehow I wedged it into the trunk and we began the drive back.

After a trip to a mall for shopping, we hit the road. I missed the turnoff to the Garden State Parkway—my preferred route from New Jersey to Connecticut—and instead found myself irrevocably committed to going over the George Washington Bridge and through the bumper to bumper miasma of the Cross-Bronx Expressway.

Even in New Jersey, the relationship began to crater as Hecuba launched into a stunning recitation of all my personality problems. She railed against my lack of fun, my rigidity, my financial concerns. Her tirade, meant to "help" me, left me dumbfounded and enraged at her arrogant presumptuousness. This was Sunday; she was staying through Wednesday morning. Could we last without me throttling her? Forget about cuddling with a stranger; could I stand the sight of her?

The monologue reminded me of the worst of past relationships. I should have simply found a cheap hotel on Route 1 in Connecticut and said, "You'll be happier here," but I lacked the nerve. Instead, I got all passive-aggressive and silent, seething at her rudeness.

She made it plain at the apartment that romance wasn't in the picture. She was happy to get my expertise for her big concern, the one that played into my male "problem solving" ego so adroitly. Social upheaval sharpened her desire to leave Farfarawayland for the United States. I had reviewed her résumé and cover letter, made some edits, and gave her ideas for people to contact in her quest for employment in the U.S. I even discussed her situation with a teacher at a local Jewish day school. Nothing came of it, but I tried.

Hecuba transformed before my eyes from the mysterious sexy visitor to an annoying Jewish female version of a character from the latest Adam Sandler movie. Nothing improved as the visit stumbled along. She probably found me equally aggravating and wimpy compared to the rugged and upscale fighter-pilot types I imagined her with. By the time Wednesday morning rolled around, I couldn't wait to transport her and her mighty suitcase and all the other junk she bought to the Stamford stop and wish her bon voyage. I've rarely been so relieved to be out of another person's presence.

I will give Hecuba credit for introducing me to the music of Senegalese singer Youssou N'Dour, especially his evocative duet with Neneh Cherry, "7 Seconds."

Chapter 12

A Week in Brazil, or, When Astral Met Peludo

When I dipped my toes into the pool of online dating, I never expected how far the search would take me—literally. In contrast to my pre-marriage dating patterns, where Industrial-age technology made me strictly a locavore, the online channel opened up the whole world. Some people take a hard line on only dating locally (being in Connecticut, I was far too distant for women clinging tenaciously to the rock of Manhattan), but my restless, dissatisfied post-divorce self stayed alert to adventures that pushed way outside my comfort zone.

Before I visited there in 2004, I knew almost nothing about Brazil. The natives liked soccer. The beaches were sandy. The Amazon was a big river. I had some Stan Getz Brazilian-themed jazz albums. That was the sum of my cultural awareness. The interest level began to change when a woman I'll call the Girl from Ipanema contacted me through an online dating site. We're both Jewish, enjoyed writing, and had increasingly friendly online chats. I called her several times and she talked about me visiting her. Because of the distance and post-divorce emotional wariness, I didn't take the offer too seriously and never considered a visit's pleasures. The Girl from Ipanema and I drifted apart and by early 2004 she turned locavore, which made perfect sense. My loss.

A few months later I contacted a woman in São Paulo. Let's call her Astral. Again, we formed a connection, as best one can online. She also invited me to visit. This time I felt more confident and eager for adventure. Instinct said "Do it," so I surprised her, myself, and most of my family by agreeing. After considerable checking of calendars and airlines, we settled on the last week in November as the best time. I wrote about my experience there for a São Paulo website, gringoes.com.

The complexities of a cross-cultural romance emerged after I ordered my tickets through my employer's travel office. Soon, the corporate security service sent a lengthy email wishing me "success and a safe voyage on your upcoming trip to Brazil." After that cheery opening, the email got down to the nitty-gritty. I was warned, for example, about: severe crime in São Paulo and elsewhere, even Guarulhos International Airport; unhealthy tap water and ice; and even "chloroquine-resistant P. falciparum malaria." Great, I thought. I'm looking for love and finding malaria.

Given that I'm a paranoid gringo when it comes to international travel, the well-intentioned warnings left me doubting the wisdom of romantic instinct. Kidnappings, airport theft, rabies; what was I getting myself into? I forwarded the alert to Astral, writing, "What do you think? I'd better not send this to my brother—he'll freak out!" (My younger brother strongly opposed this 5,000 mile jaunt to visit a woman I'd never met in another country).

Astral replied with a light-hearted note, saying, "The only serious advice I have is that you get the best health insurance you can just in case you collapse after meeting me. And also, just in case I kidnap you to the best places in town just have plenty of valid credit cards! Now, if you wish to go to the jungle in the Amazon rainforest, then get all those vaccinations, darling."

Still, my concerns deeply offended her. My frame of reference for Latin America stopped thousands of miles away from Brazil. I grew up on the Texas-Mexico border, and past visits to Mexico and El Salvador merely led me to interpret Brazil in terms of those countries. "Brazil is not El Salvador," she told me, exasperated at my ignorance. Even a week before I left I was asking my doctor about shots I might need. My plan to carry my passport, travelers checks and other papers in a Velcro-sealed travel pack around my neck didn't impress her, either.

Oh, to hell with it, I finally thought. I didn't take the shots, I didn't buy extra insurance, I simply left Astral's phone numbers and my flight plans with my ex-wife and my brother. Then I boarded the Saturday night American Airlines flight and stumbled out the next morning into that hotbed of criminality, Guarulhos Airport.

My Brazil experience had a slow but uneventful start. I snaked through passport control and customs, joining the special Yankee line to be fingerprinted and photographed. After a long haul I finally emerged into the terminal and had my first sight of a fresh and happy Astral in a delightful white business suit. She soon found a Portuguese nickname for me, practically a requirement in Brazilian culture: Peludo, or "furry."

The next week very much reflected Astral's Brazil, neither a typical tourist experience nor a long-term expat's view. I'll draw a modest curtain over most of our personal interactions, more suitable for a novel than this book. Some highlights:

Food

We visited Baby Beef, a crowded, delectable food experience, everything the travel books suggest. What I remember in even more detail is lunch on Saturday, on our way in from the airport, at a Japanese sushi restaurant downtown. Dazed from the long flight, the slog through customs, and the sheer novelty of a new city and a new friend, I think of that place as my real introduction to Brazil. A Japanese man entertained the crowd by singing American pop songs by Neil Diamond, Billy Joel and others, accompanying himself on guitar. Astral said he didn't actually speak English. American music by a Japanese man in São Paulo: in a word, surreal.

Traffic

The congestion in São Paulo was horrendous—no surprise. What surprised me was the round-the-clock bicycle traffic in Guaruja, a beach town. The flocks of bikes added a graceful, quiet note to the place and helped keep traffic congestion down. I even saw dozens of bikers after midnight, on the short ferry ride from the city of Santos to Guaruja. The sturdy, practical bikes were a welcome contrast to the fashion-statement mountain bikes so popular in the U.S.

On the beach in Santos, Brazil, in a Princeton reunions shirt.

Santos

Friends of mine who had lived in Brazil and visited Santos collapsed in shock when I sang the praises of sophisticated Santos, based on a seven-hour day trip for beach, shopping, and dinner. "Santos? When I was there, it was a dump!" exclaimed one. All I can say is that they saw one Santos, I saw another. The wide swooping beach with rocks rising from the sea proved a perfect backdrop for photos. The endless apartment buildings along the shore drive were majestic in their variety and testified to Brazilians' skill at constructing massive numbers of housing units (I'm talking about the outward quantity and appeal to a U.S. apartment dweller; I have no idea about the interior quality). A few blocks inland, in the buzzing business district, we made our major touristy buys: Astral selected two CDs of *música popular brasileira*, or MPB, for me (*Agora é que São Elas* and *Gilberto Gil Unplugged*), while I got two pair of shoes.

Marketing

The weekend street-level marketing teams for upscale dwellings delighted me. Young women in coordinated uniforms touted developments by passing fliers through car windows and unfurling banners in front of stopped traffic at red lights. I've never seen this kind of selling in the U.S. I even saved two fliers as marketing mementos of São Paulo: Loft Ibirapuera and Townhouse Village Morumbi.

Hebraica and Chabad

The Jewish Community Center in São Paulo amazed me with its size, level of services, and friendly spirit. It stood like an oasis plopped behind (very) secure walls in the center of urban tumult. From the swimming pools to the library to the movie theater to the art gallery to the simple pleasure of strolling and greeting friends, Hebraica offered everything a close-knit community needs in a central location. It may not merit mention in general tour books, but for Jewish travelers, Hebraica is a must-see. If I lived in São Paulo for any length of time, I'd join. I also attended a Shabbat service at a Chabad synagogue, where the rabbis knew the rabbis of Chabad branches I had visited in Connecticut. Years later I attended a seder with Chabad of Burlington, Vermont, where one of the rabbis was from ... São Paulo. It's a small rabbinical world, after all.

Language

The smoky bingo parlor in Guaruja suggested a great way to study numbers in Portuguese. Listening to the bingo callers, I connected what I heard to the numbers posted on the big display board. I got a double reinforcement: hear it and see it.

Entertainment

Before I left for Brazil I was already addicted to Latin telenovelas, mostly Mexican soap operas. The theme music always rocks, the star actresses are *muy caliente*, and, anyway, I could justify watching anything as a way to improve my Spanish. I had always heard Brazil does novelas better than anybody, so Astral introduced me to one of the favorites, *Senhora do Destino*. My best memories of the trip involve nights in Guaruja, sprawled on a beanbag chair after a day on the beach, watching *Senhora do Destino* while Astral translated. The theme music especially struck me, with its haunting, soaring vocal. The music stayed with me long after I returned. I couldn't remember the performer, and Astral and I were no longer in contact. Then one evening I was listening to an Internet radio service and the unmistakable riff came on. I immediately checked the information and found it was Maria Rita's magical performance of "Encontros e

Despedidas." Within a week I had ordered her CD from Amazon, along with a Bebel Gilberto CD. Their music always transports me to summer nights in Guaruja.

Brazil got under my skin. A brief reality mixed with ongoing fantasies to create an interest that deepened over the years, although the relationship with Astral didn't flourish after the trip.

Music led the way, from the first CDs I bought in Santos to a solid knowledge of bossa nova and the work of other performers: Maria Rita, the late Tim Maia (who combined Solomon Burke-style American soul music with Brazilian beats, to great effect), Robert Frejat, Celso Fonseca, Seu George and many others. I've been to the Bossa Nova Brunch at S.O.B.'s in New York and recently heard Gal Costa, a star singer for forty years, at Carnegie Hall. My subscription to the Pandora music service typically tunes in to Brazilian artists; for variety, I'll listen to mpb.com.br, a station that the Girl from Ipanema recommended. Lately, I've been exploring the Brazilian music found on the Spotify online service. Seriously, I listen to more music in Portuguese and Spanish than I do in English. With a dictionary I can translate most of the lyrics.

As an inveterate language nut, I listened to Portuguese tapes and CDs for years. I finally decided to make a bigger commitment, and one summer I took six weeks of intensive Portuguese at Brazil Ahead in New York, four days per week. Despite years of ragged self-study, I could barely keep up with the class, especially the listening part, but I gamely stuck with it and may start again. My favorite learning moments involved, of course, music. The class introduced me to the group Tribalistas, which brought together singers Marisa Monte, Carlinhos Brown and Arnaldo Antunes. I had heard of Monte and Brown, but didn't know Tribalistas. The teacher played one song, and I was hooked. I had to get that album. I found it, listened to it, loved every cut and could play some of them five times—like the first song, "Carnivalizar," and "Já Sei Namorar"—without getting tired of them. The album bewitches me with its interplay of voices and musical styles.

On the film front, I've worked my way through most of the Brazilian DVDs at the local library. I liked them all, especially *House of Sand, Alice's House, Bus 174, City of God,* and the TV series *City of Men.* I follow the economics and social issues of the country as best I can from a distance, and keep up with local happenings through the Brazilian newspapers published in the New York area that I can find around the Little Brazil neighborhood on West 46th Street. A friend loaned me the novel *Tieta*, by Jorge Amado, warning me that it was "spicy," and I read as much as I could before its length exhausted me.

I've thought about returning. I'd like to see Rio de Janeiro. My interest remains strong, although no longer tied to Jewish online dating. Still, those online connections—multiple ones, in Brazil and in the U.S.—struck a chord that continues to resonate. Every time I hear "Encontros e Despedidas" and "Carnivalizar" and "Eu Amo Você" ("I Love You" by Tim Maia), images and memories swirl in my mind, some that really happened, others simply unrealized hopes tied to a gamble 5,000 miles away.

So, all that's left to say is: Obrigado, Astral.

Chapter 13

The Birth of Longing, or, A Baptist Chick in a Halter Top and Other Images

After reading this far, you must be thinking: How did this guy get to be who he is? He's so—off-kilter in some ways. How far back can his quirkiness be traced? Well, putting aside the First Baptist Church of Mission, Texas, for the moment, let's talk about the growth of my awareness of the carnal side of life.

I confess: my favorite erotic aroma is chlorine. I can't resist its siren odor. Chlorine imprinted itself on me as a preteen and I never escaped.

I thank Mrs. Walsh for this. Mrs. Walsh held swimming classes every summer at the pool of the Fontana Motor Hotel in Mission. The pool reeked of chlorine, which clung to me and wafted around the whole complex. I could even smell it in the Fontana's lobby, where I wandered after class.

Ever the curious reader, I checked out the magazines in the lobby's gift shop. There I found *Playboy*. Golly, I thought, this is a change from *Hot Rod* and *Dave Campbell's Texas Football*. Even then, I knew an eleven-year-old shouldn't really be scanning *Playboy*, so I slipped the magazine into another one—male readers know this drill. I flipped through the issue, trying to look nonchalant. But Misses June and July dazzled me with their undraped allure and bubbly smiles.

Case in point: I still swoon for July 1969 cover girl Barbi Benton, AKA Barbara Klein. In the unpainted passageways of my brain, the Fontana's chlorinic aroma mixed with this vision of Barbi on the beach. A whiff of chlorine returns me to July, 1969—those eyes, those shoulders, Barbi's brown hair tumbling down her curving waterslide of a back. In a flash I'm back in the Fontana's lobby, where Mrs. Walsh's class ended and my introduction to another wet side of life began.

Forty years ago, I had to figure these things out on my own. With no Internet, no cable TV and no older sibling, I had few outlets or role models to answer questions or help me scope out "sexy." My mother wasn't much for talking about the changes of adolescence, and my father moved away after they divorced in 1962, playing no role until I was a teen. I couldn't look to the larger community for guidance. Mission shared the conservative culture of deep south Texas, where you didn't discuss adolescent sexuality or liberal politics.

That was the surface. Peer beneath, and you'd see that the place throbbed with all the hormonally driven drama of any town. I knew about affairs and busted marriages; forbidden passion in Mission's grapefruit groves and the teen pregnancies that sometimes resulted; the tears when parents wouldn't let their kids date a Mexican (or a gringo, as happened to me); big talk about Boystown, the red-light district in Reynosa, Mexico, on the other side of the Rio Grande. I even heard—very quietly—about gays and a reputed gay bar in McAllen, that wicked metropolis east of Mission. The McAllen *Monitor* carried ads for the Rio Grande Valley's own adult theater, the Capri in Edinburg, which touted itself as "where the elite meet."

My dear late mother blessed me with her salty and accepting take on life. She would show my brother and me mimeographs of ribald jokes and drawings that circulated at her insurance-agency office. I'll always treasure her comment upon hearing of the betrothal of an exceptionally prim young woman from the First Baptist Church of Mission. She observed, "Hmmm, I guess she'll do it by the Book."

Against this background, I stumbled step by step toward what I liked. Some of the images made a deep impression, as those memories of Fontana afternoons attest. Compared to the visuals available today—Facebook, instant messaging and the hook-up culture—my thrills were mild. But they were mine.

The actual mechanics of sex and bodies embarrassed me. Our pediatrician provided my brother and me with booklets on male and female maturation when I was around ten. Drawings showed the parts and process and where Plug A enters Socket B. I avoided the materials because they forced me to acknowledge what bubbled in my id; I couldn't see those thoughts as normal. The booklets were about body chemistry, parents making babies and wet-dream reality, not the girls around me and unvoiceable fantasies. I shoved the booklets into the closet under a stack of *Saturday Evening Post* magazines.

I groped through the ways of the world on my own. Insights came from surprising sources. For example, to this day I believe that Tom Sawyer is one of the most suggestive books ever written. Twain expressed my inchoate longings, bubbling up and around me when I noticed the early developing girls at William Jennings Bryan Elementary School.

I quoted *Tom Sawyer* in the *Nassau Herald*, the senior yearbook at Princeton University, where new graduates at age twenty-two sum up their life philosophies. While others turned to Bruce Springsteen and Virginia Woolf, I invoked Mark Twain. The passage I selected involved Tom Sawyer and Becky Thatcher: "In a little while the two met at the bottom of the lane, and when they reached the school they had it all to themselves. Then they sat together, with a slate before them, and Tom gave Becky the pencil and held her hand in his, guiding it, and so created another surprising house. When the interest in art began to wane, the two fell to talking. Tom was swimming in bliss. He said, 'Do you love rats?' "

I probably read *Tom Sawyer* when I was ten years old, in 1967 or 1968. Re-reading this passage, I can relive exactly what captured my attention. Tom and Becky are alone, they talk, they touch, he's thrilled at the intimacy, and then he says the wrong thing at the wrong time about old flame Amy Lawrence (boys do tend to stick their foots in their mouths, and girls do like to point this out). Later passages touch on anger, jealousy, complications from other relationships, reconciliation and emotional support in life-threatening difficulties. Far more explicit writings from "adult" novels merely embroider these primal themes.

When Tom and Becky are trapped in a cave, the erotic overtones are darker and more urgent. What will Tom and Becky do in a deadly situation? "Tom kissed her, with a choking sensation in his throat, and made a show of being confident of finding the searchers or an escape from the cave." Any moonstruck boy can extrapolate the scenario to play the plucky hero earning a kiss.

When you're ten years old, your mind begins to run riot, but it can only go a certain distance. That distance stretches out as you age. How often as an adult have I acted out Tom's bravado, vowing, "I'll save you!" in a mad effort to lead a woman from her dark place and win her love?

Action films had a huge impact at an early age. The rambunctious romantic Tom Sawyer grew into adulthood with new personae, as James Bond, or a zombie destroyer, or a soldier. And a curvaceous all-grown-up Becky Thatcher always brightened the picture. Certain scenes replayed in my mind for decades.

How accurate are my memories? I recently rewatched the movies with adult images that grabbed me. In each case, I remembered how they hit me right where my hormones begged to be hit. First came *Dr. No*, the earliest Bond movie with Ursula Andress as Honey Rider rising from the sea in a bikini. This film came out in 1962 and I must have seen a re-release years later. Andress looked lovely in her bikini, of course, but what really wowed me was the scene of Bond sucking sea-urchin poison out of Honey Rider's foot. *So that's what a man does!*

Other powerful images appeared in *The Blue Max* and *The Omega Man*. Each movie showed men and women in extraordinary circumstances. The action gave me a rationale for watching the movie, and the erotic parts were the icing on the adolescent cake.

The Blue Max involved German fliers in World War I. It starred George Peppard and (again) Ursula Andress as his married lover, Countess Kaeti von Klugermann. In my notes from watching the video, I wrote,

> Plunging neckline, only woman in a world of gray men and uniforms, pink nightgown and schnapps, 'horrible, but quite stimulating,' teasing him, brazen. He unties gown, she pulls it off, view from armpits up, everything in shadows, silky Bernard Herrmann score. Naked back, towel around waist, then breaks, startling, unexpected, glimpse of edge of breast, kiss. Unrealistic (towel part), incredible back. Tears up prettily.

The titan among early teen erotica, no question about it, was *The Omega Man* from 1971, with Charlton Heston as the zombie-battling Dr. Robert Neville, cruising post-apocalypse Los Angeles. It featured Neville's sizzling interracial love affair with another survivor, tough-talking soul sister Lisa, played by Rosalind Cash. Not only did I see plenty of Lisa, but I heard dialogue with sexual bite. *So this is how men and women talk*, I thought in the darkness of Mission's Border Theater. My breathless notes said,

> Her back—quick. A little breast on side, ass, back, lots of shadows. 'You haven't lost your bedside manner.' 'Is that so?' She's getting planned parenthood supplies, laugh as they get birth control pills, look at each other, then they dress like they're going to a cocktail party. Trying on clothes, in panties, holding them up, like getting zapped on the head for a thirteen-year-old!

Images were one thing; translating curiosity into reality was another. That began to happen, by the bye, at Mission Junior High School and its sock hops, along with boy-girl parties. Goodbye piñatas, hello slow-dancing to Chicago's "Color My World."

Teen lust and conservative religion mixed together in one head-zapping image. In the summer of 1972, the youth group at the First Baptist Church, which I then attended, welcomed a new member, a girl whose family had just moved to town. Since I once described her as "Venus in jeans," let's call her Venus. My very first glance of her struck me dumb: she was fourteen, with curly red hair, in a halter top. A halter top! This was reality: I could actually see her uncovered skin. Countess von Klugermann stepped off the screen and verily was made flesh. This vision of a Baptist chick in a halter top marked the first time that I moved from reading about Tom Sawyer to wanting to act like Tom Sawyer. I yearned to get to know Venus in ways the First Baptist would not officially approve.

Venus and I dated on and off through Mission High School and even beyond. We had our dramas in the hallways, and I bumbled along, more rebuffed than encouraged. The halter-top introduction was the most I ever saw of Venus. I constantly said the wrong thing at the wrong time and got "ragged out" for that, as the local phase went.

While Venus and I veered between mildly making out in my mother's 1968 Chevy Impala and ignoring each other, movie images changed. I remember the visuals, but also the emotional tones. I was learning that eroticism and sexual longings involve vulnerabilities and feelings, not just rescuing damsels from mutants.

I saw *Jeremy* in 1973, with Robbie Benson and Glynnis O'Connor. Set in New York, it detailed the relationship between music nerd Jeremy and new-girl-at-school Susan. Jeremy sees her and pines for her. The movie perfectly depicted the yearnings and possibilities of high school lust and connection. Rewatching the movie, I am struck by the dialogue, which is exactly right for characters I identified with. The sexual tension mounts and the two find themselves alone on a rainy afternoon at Susan's apartment. The music swells, Jeremy removes his glasses, fumbles with her bra strap. Susan takes matters in hand and removes her sweater and unhooks her bra. His hands are on her back, he kisses her nose, and nature takes its course. What struck me even more, in retrospect, came after the lovemaking, when Susan brushes her hair and takes a bath with what I noted as "post-coital mooniness."

In a taxi afterward, the conversation captured the after-the-fact uncertainty and anxiety that adults also feel in these moments: he asks if something is bothering her, and she replies she just feels "wispy."

She later tells Jeremy how she could still feel him "all over my body."

Heady stuff. Beyond the seminude scene, the characters' rampant emotions also connected with me, as we were all lonely teens reaching out, yearning for a special someone, ready to kiss and stroke and have something "serious," as Susan tells her father about her relationship with Jeremy.

As a budding writer, I also delighted in the written word. Once, I was at a paperback display with a friend and I idly flipped through *The French Lieutenant's Woman* by John Fowles, published in 1971. With blind luck, my eye fell on the book's hottest scene, in which, somewhat like Susan and Jeremy, fallen woman Sarah keeps the action rolling with stuffy male character Charles. As found on page 313 of the hard cover edition, in Fowles' mock-Victorian prose, Charles reaches into Sarah's and finds "forbidden female flesh, silken and swollen contours." Well! That fired my teen imagination.

I nudged my friend and said, "Hey, look at this." I showed him the steamy passage.

"Wallach!" he exclaimed.

I would not read the full passage or the whole book for over thirty years. Only in 2005 did I realize that, when it comes to "forbidden female flesh," we guys sometimes react in unintended ways. While Tom Sawyer and Jeremy managed their erotic interludes well, poor Charles, well ... I winced at his reaction: he vomited next to Sarah's head. Yech.

By 1975 my movie viewing had advanced to seeing the erotic spoof *Flesh Gordon* with friends. The plot involved the evil Emperor Wang of the planet Porno and his diabolical "sex ray." I can't remember any sex scenes, but bits of the script stayed with me, as in the song lyric about Emperor Wang, "Without him the planet Porno would be oh so forlorno." *Paradise Lost* it's not, but the line scans well and has a clever ring to it—why else would I remember it almost thirty-seven years later?

One last film stands out, at the end of an arc of my growing awareness of the often-messy flip side of sexuality. I saw *Shampoo*—starring Warren Beatty as horndog hairdresser George, with Julie Christie as Jackie and Goldie Hawn as Jill, as two of his objects of lust—when it debuted in 1975. Something about the movie haunted me. I gazed on Julie Christie's slinky, revealing gowns and saw Goldie Hawn in panties and a baby-doll nightgown, and the movie sizzles with raunchy talk, but the shock came elsewhere. I couldn't identify it. Upon another viewing at the age of fifty-one, I got it. *Shampoo* trembles with female emotions, as George beguiles and then betrays one woman after another. Jackie and Jill's raw feelings of wanting and hurting scream off the screen.

The emotional climax comes when Jill stumbles upon George and Jackie having sex on a kitchen floor. Seeing them through a window, an enraged Jill throws a chair through the window, screams "You bastard!" and runs past them, while Jackie sits disconsolately on the floor. Jill's pain is terrible to watch, and we wince at her line to George: "I'll know you're incapable of love and that will help me."

Frantic George veers back to Jackie and pleads, as men through the ages have pleaded, for her to take him back, crying, "I'll make you happy, I swear to God I will."

Jackie falls to her knees, distraught. "It's too late," she says.

The women were sexy and the language was risqué, but what I truly remember about *Shampoo* is, "you bastard" and "it's too late." Tom and Becky grew into Jeremy and Susan and crashed into George and Jill and Jackie.

Nothing like Jeremy and Susan's rainy-day interlude ever happened with that Baptist chick in a halter top. She made sure of that. All these images remained cerebral, untested theories. My own sentimental education remained maddeningly pure. Had the opportunity to act on impulses arisen, I don't know how I would have reacted.

Actually, I do know.

First, some background. My brother and I traveled to New York to see our father in the summers of 1972 and 1974, and I went on my own in December 1974 and the summer of 1975. Our father relentlessly sought to remake my brother and me from untutored "cowboys" into Brooks Brothers-clad, opera-appreciating Upper East Side gentlemen. He expounded for hours on our pathetic educational, social and cultural state.

In August, 1974, Dad and his wife (he remarried in 1962) took us to Miami Beach, where his parents were celebrating their fiftieth anniversary. There, in the lobby of the Montmartre hotel, he decided that the perfect moment had arrived to give us the big sex talk. As we sat in the lobby, Cooper and I listened, and he gave us his views of the world of the sophisticated man. His tour of sexuality's far horizons touched on brothels, nudist camps, STDs, masturbation, the Oedipal complex, the value of backseat quickies and much more. My ears perked up when he advised us "to have a sexual encounter with an older woman to teach us all about what women like."

(I recounted this monologue in my journal and, after several hundred words, wrote, "This may be an incredibly understated news flash, but Nixon resigned yesterday.")

In the summer of 1975 I returned to New York alone for college interviews and to take short-story and photography classes at the New School. Cooper had had more than enough of our father's "you uncultured Texas hicks" attitude and stayed in Mission. But the bright lights of the city beckoned and so, wary as I was of my father's bullying, I headed to New York and hoped for the best.

Dad decided to make his Montmartre theories into my Manhattan reality. In his typical manner, he steered me to the toys and games section of Bloomingdale's to announce his big plan: he had arranged for me to spend the night with the thirty-five-year-old "physical therapist" of an antiques dealer pal of his. He wanted to extend his control into the most intimate, sensitive parts of my life.

I wrote,

> I was floored. Pow. All my fantasies ... are mine—once—for the asking. Frankly, I've had little else on my mind. I can do IT.

The offer tempted me but I quickly declined. Whatever the appeal of fantasies made flesh, I absolutely would not allow my father to be my pimp. I refused to give him any say in this matter. His wife told me the woman was very nice, but I dug in my Texas boot heels and would not reconsider. To this day I have no doubts about the rightness of my decision—I was seventeen and horny, but I also had my self-respect and emotional independence to consider. I would rather keep my virginity than lose my sense of self to my father's overbearing demand to shape my life according to his values. (He also told me, "Van, they'll eat you alive at Princeton if you don't know opera.") For this and other reasons, the summer was a disaster.

So my grand chance to act on impulses came and went, unconsummated. After I returned to Texas, this brush with erotic reality left me exhausted and bored with sexy imagery. In August 1975, while checking out the University of Texas at Austin, I saw *Last Tango in Paris*. The film did nothing for me; I don't remember a single moment of it and have no interest in seeing it again.

My relationship with Venus became ever more exasperating for both of us. We saw, yes, *Shampoo*, at El Centro Mall in McAllen and I wrote that "we were thoroughly mad at each other, just like the good old days." I had already seen the movie in New York, so I knew what was coming. We held hands until the scene when Goldie Hawn's Jill throws the chair through the window. As I reported, I turned to Venus and whispered, "There she goes again, always over-reacting!" Venus, really steamed, withdrew her hand for the rest of the flick.

It had come to this: the Baptist chick in the halter top watched George, Jill and Jackie with me, and I left the theater feeling just like George in *Shampoo's* last scene: alone in the world.

I carry an updated mental list of post-teen sexy images. The older I get, the more I prefer not so much specific scenes in movies or books, but rather a suggestive mood, an appeal to my imagination. The way I describe it, the women on MTV are raunchy, the women on Country Music Television are alluring. Lately, I've become an enthusiastic fan of *The Good Wife* on TV, where I gaze in hushed awe at star Julianna Margulies as she shifts from business-suit prim and professional to volcanically aroused in most episodes. Forget Kim Kardashian and her ilk—give me Julianna in her power suit.

Finally, to give the devil his due, as an adult I found that some of my father's ideas from the Nixon Summer of 1974 weren't half-bad after all. I just had to explore them in my own sweet time, even if I had to wait thirty or so years. Which one? A hint: car-nal knowledge.

Chapter 14

The Sexiest Jewish Movies, or, Melanie, Amy, Lena and Beyond

In the previous chapter, I wrote about how books and especially movies shaped my perceptions of life from an early age. Like other American kids in the '60s, I soaked up rugged images from John Wayne movies at the historic Border Theater in Mission, Texas. Then I started noticing the curvaceous Bond Girls as fantasies.

As an adult, the movies of Woody Allen showed me an urban, Jewish take on life. My dating career always had an urban comedy air to it, with scenes of Passover-seder angst that could have been lifted from Allen's works. Actresses such as Melanie Mayron, Barbara Hershey (AKA Herzstein, with a Jewish father) and Amy Irving helped define the look and spark I yearned for in a Jewish woman.

From decades of attentive film-going, I distilled a list of the sexiest Jewish movies and stars. Granted, some of the actresses aren't Jewish, nor are the roles, but that's not going to interfere with a good idea. This idea came to me when I was thinking about "Best of" movie lists. A well-circulated list of the top fifty Jewish movies ranges from heartwarming to harrowing, *Fiddler on the Roof* to *Schindler's List.* Yet nobody has ever analyzed Jewish cinema through the filter I prefer: the *Sexiest* Jewish Movies. That's a big cultural omission, since sensual zest has permeated Jewish life at least since the writing of "The Song of Songs."

I decided to fill this gap in cinematic analysis.

What are Jewish movies? I define a Jewish movie as one where the characters identify as Jewish and take that identity seriously. Such movies may or may not deal with "religion" as such, but the identity colors characters' lives and history. That eliminates movies where characters reek with self-loathing and treat their identity as a burden, or where Jewishness functions merely as a shorthand way to declare, "I'm hip! I'm edgy! I'm neurotic!" My Hall of Shame category here deals with that nonsense.

What makes films erotic? Eye candy counts—getting to view hot Jewish bodies—but I also like the way characters act, their personalities, their seductiveness and ability to draw me into a situation. The sexiest body part, as we all know, is between your ears, so if a movie hits me there, it qualifies. Explicitness doesn't always work; Lena Olin in a bowler hat in *The Unbearable Lightness of Being* dazzles me but I am repelled by Kate Winslet as a clothes-shedding death-camp guard in *The Reader*.

Obviously, this list reflects the views of a fifty-something straight male. I mostly list films plucked from distant memory, although I've seen several recently and rewatched two of them to check whether my first impressions were accurate (they were). Besides favorite films, I've also included several Lifetime Achievement Awards to honor those performers with an outstanding body of work that I've enjoyed for decades. So, the envelopes please ....

Jeremy is a Robbie Benson coming-of-age film. I've already mentioned that I saw it as a teen when it debuted in 1974, when I was the same age as the characters. He's a nerd from New York, and dancer/love interest Susan is a creative soul who's new in town from Detroit. He's Jewish, she's not, and how he got the last name of Jones is addressed in their conversations. Jeremy's religious background is part of the movie's tapestry, just as coming to terms with my Jewish background was becoming a major issue for me at the time. The aching sincerity and fantasy fulfillment of Jeremy and Susan going all the way gave the movie a power that remained strong when I watched it again, thirty-five years after it debuted.

Girlfriends: Before *thirtysomething*, Melanie Mayron starred in this 1981 film about a struggling Jewish photographer named Susan Weinblatt pursuing love and a career in New York. At the time I was a struggling Jewish writer pursuing love and a career in New York with about as much success. "Susan" chases men, cries, talks to Rabbi Gold—played by Eli Wallach (no relation, except in the general Member of the Tribe sense)—and in one too-brief scene exposes her ripe young Yiddish rump for the camera. I adored her and her stunning mop of dark curly hair. Even the act of watching the movie intersected with my personal life; I saw it with one of the first women I ever dated steadily in New York, Adina. The movie is not on DVD and, as far as I can tell, was only available briefly on VHS. Who's keeping the rights locked up? The reissue would be a hit.

Lifetime Achievement Award I: curvaceous Lainie Kazan (AKA Lanie Levine from Brooklyn). My fixation started when I saw her in *Playboy* in the early 1970s. Known for her cleavage as well as her singing, she appealed to me back then when my mind was young and malleable. By the time I noticed her in movies like *My Favorite Career*, *Beaches* (starring the luscious Barbara Hershey), *My Big Fat Greek Wedding* and more recently *Don't Mess with the Zohan*, her ripeness had evolved into double-plus-zaftig dimensions, but her confident, charge-ahead attitude always grabbed me. Even in her late sixties, she was getting it on with Adam Sandler in

Zohan. We should all be so energetic.

The Secrets: This Israeli movie is set in a women-only Orthodox yeshiva in Sfad, the home of mystics and Kabbalah. The mix of clashing personalities, feminism in a regimented environment and unvoiced, smoldering passions makes this movie a spiritually elevated, shabbat-observing version of a 1970s Pam Grier babes-behind-bars prison epic. In this hothouse environment, romance blossoms for two of the women, Naomi and Michelle. They circle around an ailing, mysterious outsider named Anouk, who scandalizes students with a stash of erotic paintings from her late lover in France. Naomi and Michelle exchange long passionate looks, they kiss, they get to know each other in the Biblical sense, and then the hearts start breaking. The movie has an eye-popping scene where the modest clothes fly off so the young and the frum can dip themselves into the ritual *mikvah* bath as part of an exorcism. *The Secrets* blends in some humor about the mating rituals of the Orthodox and the requisite funeral and wedding found in all self-respecting Jewish movies.

Europa Europa: This movie stands alone in its use of circumcision as a plot device and dramatic tool. It details the true story of a Jewish boy, Solomon Perel, who passes as an Aryan and even winds up in a Hitler Youth training program. *Europa Europa* haunted me with its plot line about a decent gay (closeted) German soldier learning the true identity of his Jewish Wehrmacht comrade. Nothing happens between the two, as I recall, but the yearning and the doubled sense of fatal concealment (one's gay, the other's Jewish) have a terrible poignancy. Other parts of the movie detail Solomon's desperate attempts to avoid revealing the sign of the covenant, which includes avoiding sex with Leni, the Nazi-admiring girl he loves. Sexual desire has never seemed as ominous as it does in *Europa Europa*.

Lifetime Achievement Award II: Amy Irving. What can I

say about Amy? Technically, she's not Jewish. Her father had a Jewish background and she was raised a Christian Scientist, so the name and look mask a non-Jewish reality. Still, from her role as Isabelle Grossman in *Crossing Delancey* to Hadass in *Yentl*, to later works *Bossa Nova* and *Traffic*, she embodied my fantasies of what I wanted in a woman.

Lifetime Achievement Award III: Lena Olin for her work in *Enemies, A Love Story; The Unbearable Lightness of Being;* and *The Reader.* I always linked these movies, especially the first two. *Enemies* and *Lightness* burrowed deep into my consciousness. *The Reader*, while visually explicit, left me cold, and the characters repelled me. *Enemies* concerns Holocaust survivors in New York after World War II; one man, Herman Broder—played by the late Ron Silver—is involved with three beautiful women. *Lightness* is set in Czechoslovakia in the '60s. *The Reader* takes place in the '50s Germany and tells the story of the doomed affair of a teen and a mysterious woman who lives in his apartment building. *Enemies* and *The Reader* have Jewish aspects (and I read both the books); *Lightness* does not, as far as I can tell. Beyond their European settings or characters, the three movies all share one radiant connection: Swedish actress Lena Olin. She's gorgeous in *Lightness* (released in 1988) and *Enemies* (1989), and then compelling in a dual role in *Reader*, released in 2008. At different times in the narrative, she plays Rose Mather and her daughter Ilana. Knowing Olin's earlier work gave her small but critical presence in *The Reader* another layer of meaning for me. Olin may not be Jewish, but I'll give her honorary status for her outstanding, passionate work in these movies.

Dreck Hall of Shame: *Amy's Orgasm*, otherwise known as *Amy's O* for prudish Americans who quiver at the very thought of the orgasmic pleasure of a young Jewish woman. Actually, they should quiver at the message of this movie, which I viscerally disliked. I place it in my "Dreck Hall of Shame" of Jewish erotica. It starts with the standard tropes of an ethnic romantic comedy—attractive young person laments inability to find a member of his or her group for marriage, then is endlessly hounded by family on this subject. In writer Amy's case, she yaps about Jewish men. Then, she gets into a relationship with a man who's not Jewish and their faiths never arise as an issue. The movie takes the easy way out—Jewishness is a shorthand for a set of personality traits and shrill family members, but it never assumes a deeper meaning in the lives of characters. When the appealing gentile man walks in the door, the convictions fly out the window.

Lifetime Achievement Award IV: director/writer/actor Henry Jaglom. Jaglom's works are, I'll admit, an acquired taste, like escargot. Henry Jaglom's movies, made by Henry Jaglom and reflecting the obsessions of Henry Jaglom and the mostly female friends of Henry Jaglom, have a weird attraction for me. A direct descendant of philosopher Moses Mendelssohn, Jaglom is a strong supporter of Israel and his films typically have at least one main Jewish character. The movies are maddening, but they cast a strong light on women's emotions and issues. Throw in the actresses' curly hair, olive complexions and cute figures, and the tumultuous atmosphere is just plain catnip for me. Titles like *Eating, Baby Fever, Going Shopping* and *New Year's Day* suggest the intense subject material. Sensuality and angst ooze from every frame. A quote from an article about Jaglom says everything you need to know to watch, or run screaming away from, his movies:

> Men have a hard time listening. In my films, you must listen. Men usually deny the internal landscape, preferring to externalize their experience. Women become involved. They explore what they are feeling.

If you can handle that view, you can handle a Jaglom movie. Twenty years ago, I was so entranced by his movies that I engineered, on rather flimsy grounds, a telephone interview with him. I was writing the "Video Stories" column for *Video Store* magazine. We discussed advertising on videos or some related issue. Although baffled by the interview request, Jaglom was a good sport and answered my questions the best he could, unable to see the stars in my eyes.

Now we've reached the climax of the list, the titles of the three sexiest Jewish movies ever made (according to me). None of them are Hollywood films; indeed, none of them are even in English. All are set in the past and have an earthy, matter-of-fact sensuality rarely found in American films.

Black Book, by Dutch director Paul Verhoeven, observes sexuality in the context of the Holocaust, and features Jewish resistance fighters in Holland. Verhoeven is one of my favorite directors, having also been responsible for *RoboCop, Basic Instinct, Starship Troopers* and the grossly underrated Las Vegas epic *Showgirls. Black Book* follows Rachel Stein—played by spunky Carice van Houten—as she struggles to survive and seek vengeance. Her main weapon is her sexual power, so, in the employ of the Resistance, Rachel dyes her dark Jewish tresses (everywhere!) to a glittering blonde to help her pass as an Aryan and penetrate Amsterdam's Nazi power structure. The movie vibrates with sexual tension. Statuesque supporting actress Halina Reijn also brightens up the screen with her own blazing presence. The movie's appeal is simple: Rachel is Jewish and she is sexual and she never forgets that she is both. Fun fact: I saw the movie with the Shabbat Seductress, discussed earlier.

German-made *Nowhere in Africa* won the Oscar for best foreign movie in 2002. Providing a different take on the Holocaust, it tells the story of a Germany family that escapes to Kenya in the late 1930s. The adults, Walter and Jettel, have a troubled marriage, but their daughter Regina thrives. The movie's sexual impact comes from just a few scenes, but they make every second count. In one, the husband and wife are walking on a rural road, and he says, "You're going to show your breasts like a native woman." With a seductive smile, she takes off her shirt and sashays down the road, seen only from behind, a basket on her head. His demand followed by her playful acquiescence would not be easily understood by Western audiences. In another, Regina, who is friendly with a Kenyan boy, declines his request that she take off her blouse now that she has entered puberty. They banter back and forth until she decides to climb a tree. Not wanting to get her white blouse dirty, she takes it off and up she goes. No mainstream American movie would endorse such a casual, accepting attitude toward teen sexuality. Nothing happens between the boy and the girl, by the way, at least not on screen. The final scene takes place near the movie's end after the war is over. The husband and wife reconcile, followed by lots of tastefully detailed *shtupping*. Jettel becomes pregnant, too, so the next generation of Jews is on its way.

And the winner is ... *Turn Left at the End of the World*, an Israeli movie set in 1968 in an isolated desert town for new immigrants, mostly from India and Yemen. Different Jewish communities clash amid a wide variety of sexual hijinks. I can honestly call it the *Gone with the Wind* of Jewish erotica. The movie opens with full-frontal nudity, setting the tone for the unblushing explorations to follow. Jews from different countries hook up, a student seduces her teacher, two girls partake in proto-lesbian Israeli folk dancing. In one sequence, a seduction-minded femme fatale daubs perfume between her breasts and on her upper thigh (gulp!), only to become the target of a bodily fluid-enhanced folk curse concocted by the angry wife of the man she seduces. Elsewhere, a teen muses to her engaged sister about "the first time." *Turn Left* stands as a great example of the earthiness of Israeli movies, where you see Jewish bodies in various states with no false modesty or coyness. The message is, "This is who we are, what we look like, and what we do." As the Hebrew phrase goes, "*L'chaim*"—"to life." In the most erotic Israeli movies people exult in their sensuality, enjoying it openly in the shadow of danger. And *Turn Left* has the greatest deathbed line ever: "I want to die with my makeup on."

Another powerful Israeli movie, 1982. Their mothers are so proud of them.

Chapter 15

Jewish Bodies in Motion

Smart, Vulnerable and Shtetl-Lovely: The Allure of Jewish Women

Over the course of my Jewish online dating career, I learned a lot about Jewish body image. Pre-Internet, I knew about the issues—overindulgence countered with obsessive exercise and eating disorders, negative stereotypes about men and women. The digital era offered fresh insight into what women think about their Jewish bodies, although almost no Jewish men ever have much to say.

In online dating, I could see the challenge women face with the struggle to combine visual appeal with modesty and sensitivity to the realities of aging, even gracious aging. If men declare they are looking for younger, or *much* younger women, on their profiles, what's a forty-something woman to do? Those who limit their photos to neck-up seem to be holding back, while only those with loads of self-confidence can carry off the swimsuit photos.

The anxiety of these women over their appearances metastasizes beyond the physical to overload Jewish male-female interactions with psychological baggage. The point was driven home for me when I read an essay in New York's *Jewish Week* entitled, "The Anger, and Allure, of Jewish Guys." Author Abigail Pickus presents a discouraging view of relations between Jewish men and women. She wrote of one male friend's attitudes:

> His litany against the fair daughters of Israel goes something like this. Jewish women remind Jewish men of their mothers. They're smothering. They're demanding. They're materialistic. Their families are too pushy and invasive and just plain, well, loud. In short: they're too Jewish. (And probably also too short.).

The article saddened and baffled me. The ill will between Jewish men and women sounds so foreign and implacable. In the small town where I grew up, I had no exposure to the experiences and stereotypes driving this rancorous divide in the Tribe. I knew no Jews outside my family, itself a heavily intermarried clan. My awkward teen passions focused on Christian girls.

Maybe I was lucky. I discovered Jewish women completely afresh, with no wonder-years negativity to distort the view. I never bought into the stereotypes or found them personally relevant. Most important, I never felt the revulsion that poisons how many Jewish men and women regard one another. Perhaps my experiences can provide an outsider's view of how to break through the barriers that keep our hearts divided.

My gentile lust ended in the fall of 1976 when I was a freshman at Princeton University. Beginning with my crush on a Jewish classmate on a pre-Freshman Week camping trip, I turned my attention, as if drawn by an irresistible Yiddish magnetic-estrogenic force field, toward Jewish women. *Adios*, Christian maidens of Mission, *shalom aleichem, shayneh maydelehs* Deborah and Janet and Sharon, Ellen and Amy and Eileen, Susan and Sarah and Shayla, Laura and Lauren and Laurie. The names tell the tale: the instant that Jewish women glided into view, they overwrote my interest in gentiles.

What's the deal? Why, after zero exposure, did I turn to and stay with Jewish women? Something about them clicked with me on a deep level. I once described a woman as "smart, vulnerable and *shtetl*-lovely." That's my highest praise for the appeal of the Jewish woman's mind, heart and body. They are all allure, and if they freshen their lipstick over a sushi dinner, I'll follow them anywhere. A Jewish man who dismisses such women as a group is, in technical terms, *meshuggenah* (Yiddish for "crazy").

So, I read Pickus from the point of view of an ardent fan of Jewish women in all their urgent, restless wonder. I see that her male friend has serious concerns about Jewish women, finding them pushy, demanding, materialistic. Sure, some women have the traits that Pickus's friend abhors. So what? Speaking man-to-man, I'd tell him: If you don't like who you're meeting, change your search criteria. Must your prospects fall within a narrow range of body types or careers? Is young, skinny and chic all that you seek? Pickiness may be the problem. Be open to the great range of Jewish women and you could be pleasantly surprised.

If you're not clicking with personality types in your area, look further afield, especially if you're young and footloose. Women in New York, Texas and Latin America can differ enormously in degrees of edginess, expectations, lifestyle and accent.

After years of pounding the online pavement, I've learned what works for me and what doesn't. For example, lawyers and real estate brokers are a poor fit, romance-wise. They aspire to another breed of man, an alpha male/Zohan beyond my income and, at 5' 5", my height. On the other hand, I've enjoyed friendships and more with graphic designers, teachers, film-makers, psychoanalysts and rabbis. They see the value of a man with creativity, a Jewish identity, archaic Southern manners and a passion for everything Jewish women are.

Jewish women are not perfect. Some are angry, and their fury often plays out as self-directed and self-destructive. I'm haunted by how one woman described herself while shoving me down a flight of emotional stairs: "I'm replaceable." Their anger eases when they feel accepted and desired for who they are. And they can push my buttons, too. Sometimes I wanted to quote my favorite line from the cable series *The L Word,* "You are a fucking heartbreaker."

What about the other issues Pickus raises? I've attended my share of raucous family Thanksgivings and seders. They can be a strain for an outsider, but if you connect with the woman, then the family comes with the package; just watch out for what you share with relatives with borderline personality disorders. If I can handle these Northeastern Jewish families—coming as I do from a Texas clan where dinner conversations focus on hunting, the Dallas Cowboys, Republican politics and ancestors who belonged to the Daughters of the Confederacy—then anybody can.

Now, about Jewish mothers. Pickus's friend says Jewish women remind men of their mothers. Another friend blames Jewish mothers for the problems of Jewish men. In my case, I beg to differ with the problem part. Any *mensch*-like qualities I have reflect my mother's influence. My mother, who died at sixty-three in 1984, was a thrifty, straight-talking insurance-agency secretary who successfully raised two sons alone, made a fantastic banana pudding and loved watching *The Dean Martin Show*. Her motto: "Be friends with everybody." To this day people fondly remember Mom as a loyal friend who knit afghans as wedding presents for every young bride in our border-town social circle. Jewish women with those traits do fine by me.

Finally, I learned first-hand how matters of appearance gnaw at potential Jewish matches. The one time I tried to set up a friend with a spirited and attractive woman, his first question was, "Is she tubby?" For the record, I sent him photos I had taken of her that showed, definitively, that she was not tubby. And I was slapped down for not being tall enough by women who exclaimed, "Oh, I couldn't date you, I'm 5' 6" and I love to wear high heels!" Okay, that was their choice. When I thought about appearances, the more Jewish-looking, the better. I just melted for what I call the "straight outta Moldavanka" vibe, Moldavanka being the Jewish quarter of Odessa. Jewish hair, Jewish bust, Jewish nose, Jewish women—I wanted it all. The call of the tribal DNA cannot be denied.

And for any woman who frets about what Pickus dubbed her "Jewish thighs," I can only quote my mother's trenchant observation on this matter: "There's more to love."

Our Hairy Jewish Bodies, Ourselves

In the photos on my various dating profiles, I was always upfront about my appearance. I never tried, or even wanted, to look like anything other than what I am.

Let's not beat around the bush. I'm that hairy Jewish guy—built more like Esau than Jacob—comics and cartoonists love to lampoon. While I'm bald on top, genetics compensated me with swirls of fur everywhere else: arms, legs, shoulders and back. I'd be a terrible criminal because I would leave curly DNA evidence everywhere I go.

The look has pleased me ever since a line of hair first ran down my chest as a teenager. I still delight to see the hair poke up at the top of my shirts, like a wash of black foam on a beach of skin. At real beaches, I shuck my shirt to stroll about in my barrel-chested Russian-Jewish glory. At my health club, sleeveless t-shirts display my shoulders and their halo of hair, which I view as a living tattoo of shapes, shadows and textures.

I grew up with positive images of body hair in the media, such as Sean Connery in his Agent 007 days and Burt Reynolds with his April 1972 *Cosmopolitan* centerfold. The hippies of the 1960s, who let their freak flag fly, gave me confidence with my own evolving body. That's just who I am, man. Impending baldness rankled me, since I knew, as the latest in a long line of bald Wallachs, I'd lose hair on top in my twenties. But that happened so gradually that I barely noticed and hardly cared.

Then, over the past twenty years or so, a new look emerged in media images, favoring shrunken-chested Euromen with less body hair than a Chihuahua. Advertising taunted my curl-enclosed physique. Ads in the *Village Voice* celebrate hair removal via laser and other technologies. The pages of *GQ* and *Esquire* glisten with images of young men of marbleized features with nothing on their hard but hairless abs and chests. A recent cartoon in *The New Yorker* by Roz Chast—an updated version of the ten plagues in Exodus—showed a girl on a beach recoiling from a man with a hairy back, under the title, "Unwanted Body Hair!"

And I'll never forget the derision heaped on the poor "40 Year Old Virgin" for his hairy chest, which drove him to a salon for a wax-and-rip treatment. Actor Steve Carell, who really did undergo this painful procedure on screen, got big laughs with his outbursts of yowls and curses, but the obvious message made me wince: male body hair equals social handicap.

The issue resurfaced recently with the furor over former New York Representative Anthony Weiner's photos to

Twitter pals. They show what must be a waxed bod—nobody with Jewish ancestry naturally looks so smoothly Scandinavian.

The negativity ate away at my confident body image like battery acid on ice cream. When I turned fifty, I noticed that I was now afflicted with "Hobbit ears," with their feathery outcroppings. Gazing into a mirror, I saw not a jolly bald Jewish guy with glasses and a goatee, but a Hebraic Quasimodo, scorned by the elegantly cruel Esmeraldas of online dating. I finally bought a Conair ear/nose/eyebrow trimmer to keep my unseemly growth in check. Even after that, the ads in the *Village Voice* took on new urgency. Did I dare abandon forty years of self-acceptance for a cleaner Weiner look?

I thought, "Surely other men deal with similar insecurities." Checking online, however, I found little serious discussion of male body issues, at least among straight men. The articles I did find sounded vague and forced. They concerned Brad Pitt envy, men with eating disorders, steroid use in pursuit of that ripped look; I read nothing compelling or even particularly relevant.

I did discover *The Men's Seder,* a project overseen by the Men of Reform Judaism that nods toward the unexplored land of Jewish men and their bodies. Topics for the Seder include

> What enslaves us as men?
> How do we evaluate success?
> What are the plagues of being a man?

According to one review, the new "plagues" include "prostate cancer, weight gain, hair loss and impotence." I can imagine the Seder discussion: "On this night we are all like unleavened bread, because we cannot rise. Farewell, my shankbone."

In my research, nothing I read about men and body image even approached the heart-rending agony found in the books, articles, seminars and conferences on women and body image. While I'm content to muse fondly on my hirsuteness, women strategize, mourn, rage, fret and commiserate over their bodies at great length.

And the intensity spirals upward when Jewish women raise the issue. Lily Rabinoff-Goldman wrote in the blog of the Jewish Women's Archive about women struggling "to conform to arbitrary and unreachable standards," resulting in negative attitudes toward themselves and food.

Writer Rachel Lucas reacted with rage after flipping through an issue of *Maxim* magazine. She wondered about the relentless and brutal self-scrutiny women apply, and how social expectations warp their self-respect and image. Women's avoidance of "having sex in bright light" flows from the insecurities.

As painfully relevant as such reflections are with regard to Jewish women they simply don't apply to men. Since men don't dare talk about these matters outside the Men's Seder ("Hey, how's your prostate hangin' these days?" or "Still hitting the Viagra for Shabbat afternoon?" are not questions that come naturally to our lips), I'm on my own to assess my status and decide how I relate to the mainstream culture and its standards for men. Would I shrivel in the white-hot presence of Brad Pitt or George Clooney? Would the Chihuahuas of *GQ* hammer me into a state of depression over my height, my baldness, my general lack of resemblance to "The Situation" on *Jersey Shore*?

I am pleased to report: no on all counts. Other than my indulgence in an ear-hair trimmer, I decided to keep accepting myself as I am. I successfully fought the urge to call one of those *Village Voice* advertisers for a wax-and-rip. My hairy Jewish body is—my physical self. I'll never deny that. I get positive reinforcement of this attitude by watching lots of Israeli movies. They're enjoyable because they show bald hairy Jewish guys doing cool things (e.g., driving tanks, *shtupping*) without a dollop of irony or self-loathing.

And lately, hairy guys are winning more respect. My self-confidence has bounced further back, Hobbit ears be damned, or, at least trimmed regularly. A friend on Facebook posted a link to a blog posting about actor Hugh Jackman and his fuzzed-up chest. I commented, "Fausta—you can rest even easier after looking at some of my profile photos. Hugh Jackman is a Euro-girlie man compared to, well, me." Men's fashion magazines show more natural, fuzzy models.

Often, I revel in the presence of men with the same look. At my gym, I've checked out other guys and vice versa, in a silent but friendly male competition to see who's got the biggest, hairiest—whatever.

I've felt deep kinship with a Chasidic man who exercises at the same time I do. Off come the black hat and suit, on go the gym clothes. Once we stood in line for a shower and I marveled at the tribal similarity. While he was heavier and older, our backs and shoulders looked identical. We never spoke but in that silent fraternity of the shower line I knew we were hairy-brothers-in-arms. We both come from the same Eastern European stock, two guys whose families crawled out of the mud of Ukrainian *shtetls* to eventually deposit their hirsute offspring in the United States, where we unashamedly maintain our burly physiques. Here are two Yids who'll never get a back waxing. Roz Chast may find us horrifying, but that's her problem, not ours.

The most satisfying and surprising affirmation of my look came way back in May 1987, when somebody went beyond furtive looks to poking me in wonder. I was attending the New Orleans Jazz and Heritage Festival then. The fun, the sun, the music and the crawfish made me groggy by mid-afternoon, so I stretched out on the ground, shirt off, hat over my eyes.

I had dozed off when I felt a finger jabbing my chest. "What on earth," I thought as I opened my eyes. I saw two young women kneeling next to me, staring.

"Why you are just the hairiest thing Ah've ever seen," exclaimed one of them, a black-haired woman who gave her name as Mona. They had come to the festival from Mississippi with a male friend for the music and to see the sights. Well, they got a sight to see in me. Mona, the chattier one, kept running her finger down my chest. I didn't mind her frisky explorations. "I bet you moan," I told Mona, but Mona was too sloshed to get my drift. I had my camera so I snapped a picture of her demonstrating what looked like a drunken Cajun-Caribbean limbo dance move. We listened to music for a while under the pounding New Orleans sun. Finally I handed the camera to their male buddy and he captured my special moment with Mississippi Mona and her friend, our arms around each other.

Chapter 16

I Believe With Perfect Faith

God Listens With Both Ears

For all the amusing stories I've recounted, the contacts made through online dating come with a serious side. The women and I have aged from our forties into our fifties; we deal with frail parents, career upheavals, troubled children, economic dislocations, and the daily reminders of our own mortality. In the face of all this, I find comfort in the rituals and beliefs of Judaism. They help me, as do fifty-year old connections to my Christian friends in Texas.

As the Christians I grew up among matured, they drew comfort from a serene faith in the existence of God and the power of prayer. This is the faith of many relatives in my intermarried family. I still find the core of their outlook to be natural and essential: God is real; prayer works. Have faith, however imperfect. Few of my secular Jewish friends think of religion in these terms and I respect their views. When people ask me what Jews believe, I simply point them to what Maimonides, the medieval philosopher wrote in his 13 Principles of Faith, beginning, "I believe with perfect faith that G-d is the Creator and Ruler of all things. He alone has made, does make, and will make all things" and ending with, "I believe with perfect faith that the dead will be brought back to life when G-d wills it to happen."

One September I put faith and prayer into written words when I visited the grave of the Lubavitcher Rebbe, Menachem Schneerson, in Queens, New York. Followers of his in the Chabad movement of Orthodox Judaism journey to his resting place, the "Ohel," (literally meaning a tent) to leave prayers asking for blessing and guidance. I made that journey for the first time before the Jewish New Year and left a prayer pleading for the health and well-being of people I care about: my son, brother, girlfriend, ex-wife, the President, family and friends. Following the tradition of the Ohel, I wrote my prayer requests on paper, then tore them up and tossed them into a vast tank before the Rebbe's grave, to mix with the prayers of thousands of others. The pieces of paper drifted down, and one piece landed face up so I could just read the words, "my son."

One friend would soon need all the prayers, Hebrew and Christian, that I could muster. Two months later, my friend Ilana told me she had breast cancer. I responded in the most natural way—I turned to both Christian and Jewish prayer traditions. After all, I thought, God listens with both ears. I wrote to what I call my "Texas Prayer Patrol"—childhood friends David, Dee Dee and Lois, my cousin Linda in Tyler—and asked them to embrace Ilana in their prayers. They leaped into their spiritual work, and continued to petition the Lord for Ilana every day.

At the same time, I also called on my Jewish faith. I included Ilana when I said the nighttime *Sh'ma*, Judaism's essential prayer: "Hear, Oh Israel, the Lord our God, the Lord is One." I also went online and dispatched another prayer for her to the Rebbe's Ohel.

This intense spiritual effort worked, as far as I know. Ilana underwent surgery with excellent prospects. I wrote her a note quoting a rabbi, "The Talmud locates God's presence lending comfort to patients by resting above their head." I added my own thought: "I had an image of the *malachim tovim*—the good angels—around you in the hospital and at home."

I know that Christian and Jewish prayers work in tandem to protect precious souls. God is always listening with His infinite ears.

Glorified and Sanctified

Recently I heard about the death of a woman I once knew named Adina. She had been one of the very first women I dated after moving to New York in 1980. I found a paid death notice in a newspaper from several years back, saying she succumbed to diabetes and breast cancer. She was fifty-one—younger than I am now.

Adina and I had a tumultuous relationship, thanks to our wildly different social backgrounds and degrees of sophistication: suburban Long Island versus small-town Texas, intense Jewish education versus no Jewish education. Still, we had a connection: we were writers and Jewish and on the prowl. Adina played an influential role in my life at the time.

Rabbi Shlomo Carlebach at B'nai Jeshurun in New York, Purim 1982.

Our shared practice of Judaism provided many of my favorite memories of our times together. We joined her friends to hear Rabbi Shlomo Carlebach sing during Purim at B'nai Jeshurun on the Upper West Side, a favored hunting ground for singles. I attended a seder with her family on Long Island on the snowy Passover of April 1982. With Adina's encouragement, I visited Israel in May 1982 and wrote about the experience for the *Forward* newspaper.

The little markers of memory accumulated over the months. I have photos of Adina at B'nai Jeshurun and with her friends Rena, Rochel and Marilyn. She sent me postcards from her trips to Israel and Peru. We called each other "Y.D.," short for "Yiddish dumpling."

For what turned out to be our last date, I stunned Adina with tickets to what I called "Bereshit," the Hebrew name for the book of Genesis—we saw her favorite music group, Phil Collins and Genesis, perform at Forest Hills Stadium in August 1982. That was the end. She called it quits after that.

Other relationships would follow (By year's end I was dating Calypso, whose story you will find if you keep reading), but as time passed I thought fondly of Adina. We parted in frustration, not anger. Four years later, on a rainy evening on the Upper West Side, we ran into each other again. We immediately had a long catch-up coffee klatch in a diner. Adina had left journalism to study social work, while I was several years into a stint as a globe-trotting freelance writer. Freed from the anxieties of stillborn romance, we shared a warmth and were happy to see each other.

"Don't be a stranger," she said in her distinctive, cigarette-raspy voice.

We never saw each other again. The next year I met the woman I would marry. The new flame burned bright and I fed it all the oxygen I had. Old flames flickered and went out.

Long after my divorce in the new millennium, I became

curious about Adina and uncovered the death notice. I mentally overlaid my life on top of her last years and wondered what type of friendship, if any, would have resulted from contact. Maybe nothing, but I like to think we would have stayed connected this time as friends with common interests in Judaism, journalism, travels to Latin America and, well, life. I had changed since we dated—becoming more at ease with myself, more Jewishly literate, comfortable in groups. In any case, I found myself aching and sorry that we had had no contact for those last twenty years. I never had a chance to say goodbye to Adina.

That's one missed farewell in a digital world that logs birth and death regularly. I would never have known about Adina's passing without the Internet. Online, the once-hidden and unfindable becomes common, jolting knowledge. Through Facebook, I read daily about the illnesses of friends' families, with prayer requests and mentions of deaths of parents, siblings and, most grievously, children. On Facebook, I learned that the son of one friend from Mission, for example, was killed in Afghanistan, bringing the war to me in a terribly personal way. We're in our fifties and older; passings happen and the pace quickens with age.

I learned about Adina's passing at the exact same time I was experiencing something entirely new in my Jewish life—a *shiva* call to a house of mourning. I had attended Jewish weddings and funerals, but had never visited a family sitting *shiva*, or mourning a death.

"Not even your grandparents?" somebody asked after I mentioned this anomaly.

"No, not even my grandparents," I said.

But a death occurred in a family close to me, an uncle of my girlfriend, and I wanted to pay my respects. I had no idea what to expect, although I knew of the traditional rituals of covering mirrors and tearing clothes.

So I visited some people I knew, the relatives of the elderly man who had died. I gave them my condolences. Some wore small black ribbons. I recognized the rabbi who conducted the service, which consisted of prayers I had heard many times before and could read and mostly say in Hebrew. This included the Mourner's Kaddish, the prayer for the dead. This prayer does not mention death but rather magnifies and sanctifies the Name of God. It begins,

> Glorified and sanctified be God's great name throughout the world which He has created according to His will. May He establish His kingdom in your lifetime and during your days, and within the life of the entire House of Israel, speedily and soon; and say, Amen.

As I looked around the room, I thought about how ancient tradition and ritual created such emotional support at a time of ultimate loss. People are not left to flail on their own in the darkness; they—we—have a way to mourn that links them to generations past and future.

The moment seemed right and as we prayed I said the Kaddish for my late friend. I had finally found a way to say goodbye to Adina, Y.D.

How is Chabad Like a Denzel Washington Action Movie?

One of the most intense spiritual experiences I've ever had came after Muslim terrorists killed the directors of the Chabad House in Mumbai, India, and other Jews in November, 2008. Here's what happened.

Once the deaths became known, Chabad of Stamford, Connecticut organized a memorial service that I attended. The service featured a video tribute to Rabbi Gavriel and

Rivka Holtzberg. It praised their hospitality in welcoming everyone to the Chabad House and their Jewish learning. During that mournful but forward-looking night, somebody compared Gavriel and Rivka to Abraham and Sarah, the first Hebrews, who welcomed angels and others into their household.

At that moment, something momentous clicked in my soul. Perhaps the speaker made this explicit point: Gavriel and Rivka weren't just like Abraham and Sarah—somehow they actually *became* Abraham and Sarah. Somehow, 4,000 years of history vanished and I saw the Patriarch and Matriarch.

What happened then—so long ago after Abraham heard the command "Lech Lecha" (get thee out) and left Ur of the Chaldees—assumed an electrifying immediacy in my life. I felt a more direct connection to my faith than I had ever known. A line ran from Abraham to the Holtzbergs to me.

These thoughts inspired me to rent a movie I had seen before and liked a lot: *Déjà Vu* with Denzel Washington as investigator Doug Carlin, unraveling an explosion on a ferry in New Orleans. What's the connection? You might ask, "How is Chabad like a Denzel Washington action movie?" I'll explain.

Washington uncovers a secret (of course) government research project called "Snow White" that enables viewers to peer into the past for short periods of time. The more he hears about the project, the more he wonders about the true nature of what he sees. Eventually he discovers that Snow White can function like a time machine. A technician tells Washington that the time machine "folds space" to link to different points, similar to a cell phone signal. In this case, the signal connects to a point in the past, not another cell phone caller. That scene exactly captured my feeling about the memorial service and the Holtzbergs. I felt a spiritual bridge open, spanning that November night and the life of the Patriarch. Abraham and Sarah stopped being distant myths of my religion, something taught, studied and filed away under "Jewish stuff" in the desk drawer of my life. They became immediately real through the selfless behavior of the Holtzbergs, who showed me who Abraham and Sarah were. Time dropped away, like in the movie. I found myself on the bridge between now and then, or, if you will, now and another now.

I am actually looking at and experiencing Abraham and Sarah, I thought. This is the way it was and the way it is.

Déjà Vu has a strong spiritual sensibility that echoes Jewish teachings. At a funeral service after the film's bombing, a preacher muses on God's will and the nature of time. He says that "whatever is has already been, and what will be has been before."

His words reminded me of the second principle of the 13 Principles of Faith written by Maimonides, the medieval rabbi also known as the Rambam, who wrote:

> I believe with complete faith that the Creator, blessed be His name, is One and Alone; that there is no oneness in any way like Him; and that He alone is our G-d—was, is and will be.

I read that to mean that time does not bind God, that He exists at all times. So I can extrapolate, in my "Snow White" moment, to see the Jewish people as a unity stretching forward and back. I don't mean that in a trite, fundraiser-declaration sense ("We are one!"). I am one point in a line pointing to the past and the future; I am personally responsible for doing what I can to sustain that line and extend it into centuries to come.

The memorial service called for Jews to rededicate

themselves to study and service, and I can connect my own insights there with other Jewish moments. These instances raise religious expression from an abstract ritual observance to an immediate, directly experienced reality.

For example, sometimes I'll imagine the Prophet Elijah—beloved invisible guest at Passover seders—riding the commuter train with me, a faithful, accepting companion. One of my favorite parts of the Passover seder (speaking of Elijah) comes with this statement, "In every single generation one is obligated to look upon himself as if he personally had gone forth out of Egypt."

Those words always connect with me. The seder vibrates with meaning at that moment, placing me at the Exodus, escaping bondage in Egypt for a new life. I can even interpret the story as my own spiritual wanderings, from beliefs imposed on me to a faith I freely accepted. I stand with my fellow Jews at that moment, part of a family that transcends time and place. Judaism then becomes our own "Snow White" machine.

Chapter 17

Double, Double, Toil and Kvetch, or, Consulting the Oracles of Romance

When I needed dating advice, I have a few sources of wisdom. In college and beyond, my mother provided basic values, boiled down to her favorite aphorism: "Don't get anybody pregnant." My father urged me to date beautiful, wealthy older women, which is easier said than done. My younger brother Cooper was always available to listen and lend me his hard-boiled Texas spin. When a relationship soured, I would console myself with the wisdom of a line in *Star Wars: The Phantom Menace:* "There's always a bigger fish."

My friend Steve, whom I worked with right out of college, gave me a great piece of wisdom after listening to my string of deluded rationalizations about staying in a bad relationship: "Van, you don't want thimbles of affection, you want BUCKETS of affection!"

Another friend, Larry From Brooklyn, specialized in advising women about me. He told one, "Don't try to pressure Van into doing something he doesn't want to do. It'll never work."

But for the detailed discussion, the late-night line-by-line close textual reading of what's going right (or more typically, horribly wrong), I always turned to women. They would listen and comment and give me their well-informed feminine perspectives. They could tell me when I was kidding myself, or when another woman was treating me poorly.

For example, the Lark and I swapped scores of emails about our romantic woes. I once wrote her, "I have a half-dozen or more women I can do things with. Quantity isn't the problem, nor, on some level, quality. One woman I've known for close to three years is eager for me to visit her abroad. I always feel I'm one woman behind in the trips I take; I go see somebody and then feel, you know, I should have gone to see X instead of Y."

After I updated the Lark on a turbulent relationship, she wrote, "Wow, it is hard to say goodbye. She clearly has you on her mind. How are you feeling about this?"

The process goes both ways. The women would also turn to me for help in penetrating the labyrinth of the male mind. I once advised the Lark, "So the Ragin' Cajun is back and horny? What a classy guy. He sure knows how to make a gal feel special. Your response was right—you're not his toy (unless that fills a gap in your life and that's what you want). He sounds arrogant and presumptuous."

One woman told me about her frustrations with repeated visits to a randy Orthodox man, who kept her out of sight of his family.

"So," I said with what is for me surprising directness, "you're good enough to fuck but not good enough to meet his parents?"

I had bilingual consultations with Simonetta, a teacher at a Jewish school in Mexico City. She wrote to me soon after I joined a now-defunct Jewish dating site, and we hit it off. After a week she informed me that she had found somebody else online so the romance angle died fast, but we stayed in touch. Our chats often dealt with languages—Spanish was her native language, English was mine, and confusion arose when we became involved with men or women who weren't fluent in our respective native tongues. I had several contacts with women in Latin America—they found me approachable and responsive, and I had grown up on the U.S.-Mexican border and had visited Mexico and El Salvador—so having a handy translator was welcome.

In fact, Simonetta and I often accessed each other's language skills in real time. A woman might lapse into Spanish in an instant-message session; I would IM Simonetta at the same time and relay phrases I couldn't understand to her, and she would give me a quick English translation. I did the same for Simonetta when she couldn't understand the full meaning of what a man wrote in English. While I couldn't translate into Spanish, I could give her my snap analysis of what the guy was getting at. The guidance must have worked; Simonetta married a man she met online and he moved to Latin America to be with her.

Simonetta also introduced me to a friend of hers, one of the few times I met a woman through the old-fangled personal connection route. After I met her friend, JJ, I sent this after-action report:

> Well, I tried. JJ and I had a very good time at a performance of the Ballet Hispanico last Sunday. I called to thank her and invited her to a Jewish salsa event in NY for last night. She finally got back to me and said she couldn't make it, and I got the sense she wasn't interested, so I won't push the matter. Too bad—I had a good feeling about her, but she must be looking for something else. Thanks for putting us together. I enjoyed the two times we were together.

The greatest oracle of them all, the one who has been listening for thirty years and has encountered almost all the contestants in my dating game, is my friend Chloe. We met in 1981 when we both lived in the same brownstone apartment building in Amity Street in Cobble Hill, Brooklyn. While we never "dated," we became close friends and confidants and frequently attended the open high holiday services at Hebrew Union College. Chloe and I intersected at key points in each other's lives, even after she moved to Florida and then Virginia. We attended each other's weddings, celebrated the births of children, supported each other during divorces, attended bar mitzvahs of our sons, mourned the deaths of our mothers, and swapped buckets of romantic advice. If my brother and I had a sister, she would be Chloe.

With Chloe the Oracle of Romance at a friend's wedding, 1984.

Chloe and I each have the ability to coolly dissect romantic situations and their potential and pitfalls—except for our own. I used to compare us to two winos clutching each other, each waving a bottle of cheap wine around while begging the other, "Don't drink that poison! It'll make you sick!" even as we swill our own rotgut of romance. In the early years of our friendship, I had my doubts about her beau, the ne'er-do-well communist bicycle messenger, while she warned me about my involvement with an Ecstasy-popping Joan Rivers-sound-alike.

To this day, Chloe appreciates advice based on my hard-won romantic experience. She says, "You told me, 'Chloe, don't have more than two dates in one day. If have more than two, then you get confused and you can't keep your stories straight and you repeat yourself.'"

Once we dove into the online dating scene, I became her profile photographer. Whenever we met I'd take some photos of her, edit them and send them to her to upload at the sites she used. I like to think the photos work, because Chloe enjoys a busy dating dance card. She always looked fetching—she has that Hungarian-Jewish bone structure that guarantees she will age well. And the photos do her justice in a medium where eye candy always gets sampled.

We're still talking, although thanks to a stable relationship the drama level in my life has ratcheted down several notches. I get Chloe's reports from the dating wars, and I mostly encourage her to get out there and stir things up. After thirty years of mutual coaching, I know she can do it.

Chapter 18

The Competitors, or, Encounters with Gentlemen of a Romantic Inclination

Relationships are often like revolving doors. One lover's coming in while another's moving out. Sometimes the two competitors wind up in the same revolving door, going around in circles. When the door spins fast enough, you can actually bump into the competition—the other man.

I'm not talking about the gay best buddy, or protective brother, or stolid co-worker. No, I'm talking about glinty-eyed male competitors, their testosterone surging in the eternal quest to slay the mastodon, steal the fire, present the polished-bead necklace, swing the virgins onto their snorting stallions and shove their DNA into the next generation.

In my dating career, encounters with other men of a romantic persuasion typically happened at the start or end of a relationship. One's the happy new guy, the other is the rejected suitor kicked into the recycling bin. I've had both experiences and much prefer being the guy on the front end.

In one relationship I played both roles. This is the story of Van and Calypso, a bewitching woman with high-octane sensuality and a high-drama expressive style, nicknamed after a passage in the late Robert Fagles' translation of *The Odyssey,* where he describes Calypso as "the dangerous nymph with glossy braids."

The Dangerous Nymph Calypso and I met in New York

through an elderly common friend who thought we would be nice friends and nothing more. I well remember my first meeting with Calypso at her apartment. She wore a tight turquoise jumpsuit (keep that attire in mind). The Judaic-hormonal connection kicked in over lingering, starry-eyed Chinese food dinners; thus began a madcap Manhattan romance. Despite being the same age as me, she carried more hard emotional baggage than I and was an expert at wrapping men (like me) around her pinky. In comparison, I still felt like the country rube who fell off the turnip truck from Princeton and landed in Cobble Hill, Brooklyn. She liked to talk about those generous but horrid men from her past in order to pressure me subtly into behaving the way she wanted. Calypso excelled at this. She could have been the sexy but conniving "bad girl" on a Mexican soap opera.

When we met, she had another man wrapped around her pinky. Let's call him Fredo. Moving in the brisk and bloodless manner of all femme fatales, Calypso dumped Fredo to be with me. This succession happened so abruptly that when Calypso took me to a party a day later, everybody expected her to show up with Fredo. And, in fact, Fredo did appear—he had been invited, too, after all.

Calypso, with her unerring sense of soap-operatic drama, introduced us.

"Hi, I'm Van," I said, manfully extending my hand.

"I know who you are," said Fredo, who was sporting enough to shake my hand rather than punch my jaw. We sat on opposite sides of the crowded living room, ignoring yet eyeballing each other.

"Just remember, you're the one I'm going home with tonight," Calypso cooed.

Navigating the peaks and valleys of this intense physical and emotional relationship was new and difficult for me. Differences of opinion led to explosive arguments when I wouldn't follow the relationship roadmap she carried in her head (this is the woman who told me, "Van, you're ONLY twenty-five but I'm ALREADY twenty-five."). And I had other pressures in life. My mother was dying of cancer, and my employer, a magazine publisher, had relocated out of New York to the Midwest. Rather than move and remain an editor with a trade magazine covering the frozen food industry, I had opted to stay in New York and start a career as a freelance writer operating out of a tin-ceilinged studio apartment in Brooklyn that I rented for $300 per month. I could find no stability—family, work and relationship all felt terribly fluid.

So, how can I describe my romance with Calypso? On the plus side, she was a sex goddess. She had great curves, superb skills in the feminine arts of clothes and cosmetics, and a verbal style rarely found outside *Letters to Penthouse.* A picture of us shows her draped around me with her head on my shoulder, Betty Boop lips glowing, a manicured hand resting on my chest, and a silken blouse perfectly in place. One Passover we made love in her girlhood bedroom in the suburbs while her mother puttered around with the seder table and welcomed guests. She looked good and smelled good and knew just what to say to drive a guy crazy. Calypso set the erotic bar very high.

But ... she was a gal in a hurry. She expected the relationship to move at warp speed, to where no Van had gone before. She had no sense of patience or boundaries and even dragged my ailing mother into the act. When I met Calypso, Mom was dying from bone cancer and living with her sister in Tyler, Texas. I visited Mom for what turned out to be the last time on Mother's Day, 1983. When I returned, Calypso declared that I didn't spend enough time with Mom. "I personalized it," she said. "If this is the way he treats his mother, I thought, how is he going to treat me?"

(My mother knew enough about the ups and downs of

my relationship with Calypso to warn me, "Van, I'm afraid she'll trap you and get pregnant."

"Don't worry, Mom, I'm not marrying anybody."

"Don't be so sure," Mom replied.)

A few weeks later, we attended an Israel Fair in Manhattan. We attended a presentation moving to Israel and she asked, in a studiously offhand manner, whether I'd go to Israel with her for several months on "vacation."

I said no, given my mother's ill health and my career shift. I had enough change happening in my life. She immediately shifted into rage mode and gave me the tight-lipped "you sorry son-of-a-bitch" look I knew so well.

She snapped, "Now I see I can't trust you as far as I can throw. You just confirmed what I thought all along. You say you love me twenty times a day and then when I bring this up you say, 'Oh, no, I want to do this alone.' "

Before long, Fredo re-entered the picture, meant to stir up jealousy so Calypso could jerk my chain and haul me into line. I'd had enough of the dramatics and ended the relationship. Calypso was shocked but she bounced back.

How did she bounce back?

By coincidence, a few days later we were going to a party at the apartment of a Princeton classmate who lived across the street from Calypso on the Upper West Side. That Saturday evening, as I approached the apartment, who did I see but Calypso, strolling arm and arm with another man—wearing the same form-fitting turquoise jumpsuit she wore the first time I met her.

At the party, my friend's wife told me that Calypso had called her to ask if she could attend the party with another man, since we had broken up. She was told, in no uncertain terms, "no." Calypso was setting up exactly the same male stare-down she had engineered between Fredo and me. This time, however, I would be the old lover meeting the new sheriff in town.

Yet for all the turmoil, Calypso unwittingly holds a unique place in my life. In all my chronicles of dating, online and otherwise, she is the only woman who ever interacted with both my mother and father; she spoke to my mother and sent her a hand-drawn birthday card, and she met my father at the Brooklyn Museum. After she learned from my Princeton friends that my mother had died in January 1984, she sent me a thoughtful condolence note, which I saved to this day in a bundle with all the other letters I received during those bleak winter weeks. Since then I have always remembered her as naughty but also compassionate. She has a good heart—we just weren't right for each other.

♥

X to me: "I won't be able to correspond anymore. I'm sorry. You have been very helpful to me. But someone sent my profile to my husband, and I do not know who it was. So I am uncomfortable talking with anyone, even though we had only a friendly correspondence. I hope you understand."

Me to X: "I'm sorry your life took this turn—I have no idea who your husband is (you were still married? Separated?). Did this cause some type of problem? Anyway, I hope things work themselves out for you. If you'd like to get back in touch, you know where to reach me."

♥

In the online era, encounters with other gentlemen of romantic intensions can also take place electronically. One woman, for example, had the strange habit of setting up three-way Yahoo instant messaging chats, involving me, her, and another man—a sort of digital competition to see whose conversation predominated. I felt marginalized, and stopped agreeing to these chat free-for-alls.

The sexual politics are intense. After another three-way

chat with people named Jack and Jill—who both lived in Toronto and whom I knew independent of each other—Jack hit me on Hotmail IM, peeved that I wasn't his "wingman" as he tried to impress Jill. He demanded to know how long Jill and I chatted after he left. I said "a while" but nothing else. Finally I said, "I have my friendship with Jill and that's that." What a churlish character. He sounded unhinged, I noted.

Usually the other man cropped up as the *coup de grâce* in a call or email, announcing that a woman has found someone else to focus on. This was always a possibility; so much of online dating happened in the dark, where you only saw a tiny corner of the process. Everything was in flux and nothing was settled until a man and woman agreed that things were settled. Until then, the hidden gears of potential romance were forever spinning and grinding and pulverizing.

That's what happened with one falsely promising contact I'll call YettaFromYonkers. Excerpts from her emails form a striking arc of enthusiasm that peaked with a Sunday stroll on New York's Riverside Drive.

1. I'm really excited about the idea of hiking. To redrop a not so subtle hint—my children will be with their father again next weekend, if you also have any time then. (April 9, 9:28 a.m.)

2. I like this picture. Where are you in it? (April 10, 7:58 p.m.)

3. Wow! That's Connecticut?! How gorgeous! You look pretty good too. I'm very partial to beards. I like the shirt too. (April 10, 8:11 p.m.)

4. I'm sorry our conversation was cut off so suddenly. The more we communicate, the more I'm looking forward to meeting you. Good night. (April 10, 9:18 p.m.)

5. On an irregular basis, a group of people here hold an alternative minyan. Maybe you'd like to check out this minyan some Shabbat, have lunch here? (April 10, 9:56 p.m.)
6. I was just rereading your profile—I'd love to get a demonstration of both your dancing skills (I've always wanted to know a man who could really dance; my parents were great dancers together), and your Russian skills (mine are rusty now)! Not necessarily simultaneously. (April 13, 7:50 p.m.)
7. Is there a good time this week to talk? Take care, YettaFromYonkers (April 13, 9:44 p.m.)
8. I'm going to be up working for a while, if you want to talk. (April 15, 9:34 p.m.)
9. I enjoyed meeting you also. Sorry about the sore feet, but wasn't it wonderful being outside?! It was quite zooey here this evening, but things have finally quieted down. (April 18, 10:19 p.m.)
10. Hi. I hope you're doing well. I just wanted to let you know that I've met someone with whom things have really clicked and I'm going to be focusing my attention there. I'm not someone who can have more than one conversation going at a time. Take care YettaFromYonkers (April 25, 11:55 p.m.)

Alas, poor Yetta, she never got a chance to experience my dancing and Russian skills (she would have learned that neither reached the level of even primitive ability).

Messages like the last from Yetta stung for a few minutes—my fragile male ego, you know—but then I shrugged them off. Honestly, I never had an emotional investment in Yetta or other women who said the same thing.

If I felt a glimmer of affection, I'd simply write back to congratulate her and say that if the situation changed, she knew where to reach me. Flipping the situation around, I've told women friends that I'm dating somebody steadily when they've asked, ever so casually, "So how's your love life?"

But sometimes rejection made me feel like I had been kicked in the head by a mule. After one such episode, I found myself brooding over the new top guy. I tried to picture him. This happened at a time when I had two obsessions. First, I was taking a ten-week course in Krav Maga, the Israeli martial arts form that focuses on butt-kicking survival in street fights, not finding your inner calm and oneness with the universe. I liked its directness. Second, I was fixated on the HBO series *The Sopranos* and the violent actions and capers of Tony Soprano colored my emotions (although not my actions). My mind spun wildly as I imagined the other man. Was the replacement tall, rich, worldly, maybe a Richie Aprile-style psycho with the edge and drama I lacked? (*Sopranos* fans will understand the Aprile reference.) WWTD—what would Tony do?

I soon tapped into my inner Tony. Tony's replacement moment came after he discovered Irina, a discarded girlfriend, was dating his politician friend, Ron. Enraged, Tony hunted them down and beat the tar out of Ron with his belt. In my version, thoughts of this woman and the new guy boiled over in class. I told my sparring partner I envisioned them together. He picked up on my anger and encouraged me to attack. "That's it! Now you're hitting!" he shouted as I pounded uppercuts into the padded shield he held.

When I calmed down, I asked myself, "Who was the real target? Another man who happened to appeal to a woman more than I did, or my own foolish quest?" I had made my own choices here, and knew what I was doing despite my better judgment. As in every other relationship, I was a volunteer, not a victim. I stopped brooding and just continued the search to be the fresh new guy coming in through the revolving door.

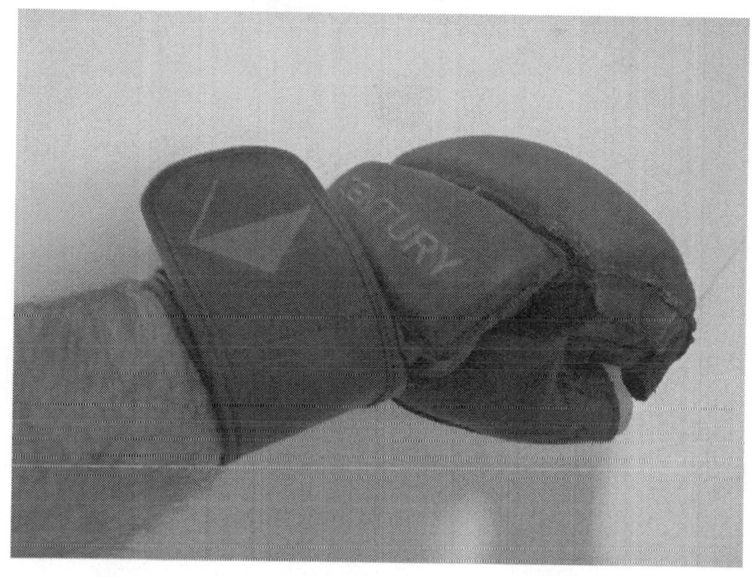

Working out my frustrations:
Krav Maga sparring glove.

Chapter 19

Beyond Online

Looking back on years of dating online, I ask myself, what did it all mean? I learned, in my roller-coastering search for romance, that being different and articulate at least helped me slide my foot in the dating door. Being from Texas was an excellent marketing tool. I also found that a thin and erasable line separates *amor* from *amoral*. I gained some great friends, slurped enough Starbucks coffee on first dates to float the Battleship *Texas* at San Jacinto, traveled to Brazil and elsewhere, endured a few sleepless nights staring at my bedroom ceiling, and was given a kabbalistic key chain from Israel that I use to this day. I had my heart cracked a few times—and I bruised several myself along the way. I'm now past the searching and its addictive qualities. I'm glad to be done with highs and lows, the endless what-ifs and juggling of multiple opportunities. The Return on Emotional Investment ultimately works better when the eggs settle in one basket.

My journeys in Judaism continue. I recently attended my synagogue's annual meeting—the first ever for me—and found it enlightening. I peered beneath the hood of the synagogue's operations, including those evergreen concerns over Hebrew school and a new building. I keep the Stone Edition of the Chumash (the whole "Old Testament," not just the five books of the Torah) at my office and start the day with a few minutes to read the *perek yomi*, or daily Bible chapter. My son and I recently teamed up to install two *mezuzot* in my apartment, following a quick rabbinical consultation to ensure we were doing the job correctly. Literally meaning a "doorpost," a *mezuzah* is a rectangular box with Bible verses on parchment. They add a traditional Jewish tonality to the place. The downstairs *mezuzah*, in the shape of a dove, was a birthday gift from my girlfriend, so it has extra meaning.

Judaism grows as part of life's rhythm. The Jewish calendar, once so foreign to me that the high holidays came as a surprise, punctuates the fall and spring seasons. Living very near Beit Chaverim, I attend services regularly—I don't describe myself as Orthodox, but I'm religious in my own way. Over decades of repetition, the services, like a meditation text, have become more familiar to me. I can read the Hebrew and follow the text, even finding my place if I lose it or, as too often happens, my attention wanders.

Moments of startling insight and even transcendence jolt me at times. During a Torah study session, a rabbi once said something that simply made total sense: "There are no days off in Judaism." That context involved observance of the *mitzvot* in Orthodoxy, but I also see it as a plan for nurturing faith as a part of one's life. Judaism is there; it's yours, if you want it. Make it matter.

My Significant Other relationship, meanwhile, has perked along for almost four years—longer than any relationship except my marriage. We've had a high ratio of enjoyment to exasperation, with a great similarity in lifestyle and values. Nothing beats an evening of Indian food and then indie music at the Tarrytown Music Hall, followed by bowls of ice cream and *Saturday Night Live*. We had a great time at the Montreal International Film Festival. Jewish activities provide memories, such as hearing Israeli singer-songwriter Idan Raichel in what we agreed was the greatest, most tribally rousing concert we had ever attended. She's always ready for off-beat adventures, such as the annual Menorah Horah burlesque show at Hanukkah and my performances at open-mic events of material inspired by this book. For my part, I gamely tag along on her visits to yarn stores and country fairs, where she spends hours sifting through hundreds of skeins of yarn to find just the right ones to satisfy her knitting addiction.

We went through many tissues watching the Holocaust movie *Le Rafle*, about the sickening roundup of French Jews in Paris in 1942. When I told her about our list of treasured memories, she asked, "What about *Dresden*?" referring to the German TV production about the February 1945 firebombing of that city. We found the drama of love and survival within the inferno quite enthralling and entertaining. Granted, *Le Rafle* and *Dresden* don't sound like traditional "date movies," but they worked for us. Setting aside our Texas-Northeast political squabbles, we're in sync on the major life issues. And when you're in your fifties, that's MECE enough for me.

Right where it ought to be: The mezuzah on the doorpost of my home.

Van Wallach is a writer in Connecticut. A native of Mission, Texas, he holds an economics degree from Princeton University. His work as a journalist has appeared in *Advertising Age, the New York Post, The Journal of Commerce, Newsday, Video Store, The Hollywood Reporter,* and the *Forward.* Van has been a regular contributor to the *Princeton Alumni Weekly* since 1993. He contributed a chapter on home-video economics to the second edition of *The Movie Business Book.* A language buff, Van has studied Spanish, Portuguese, Russian, Yiddish and Hebrew, although he can't speak any of them. His travels have included Australia, New Zealand, the USSR, Northern Ireland, Mexico, Cuba, El Salvador, Brazil, Israel and the usual parts of Europe.

You can find Van online at:
wallach.coffeetownpress.com

Made in the USA
Lexington, KY
15 April 2012